Prize M

Quincy Wright

Alpha Editions

This edition published in 2024

ISBN 9789362519955

Design and Setting By
Alpha Editions
www.alphaedis.com
Email - info@alphaedis.com

Contents

INTRODUCTION.

The rules for disposing of the proceeds of prizes captured in war is a question of municipal law. After a prize has been legally condemned, international law has no direct concern with the ultimate disposition which the captor state may choose to make of the proceeds. Indirectly, however, the prize money laws of different states may be of great interest to other states, for the character of the internal regulations in this matter may determine the amount of energy displayed by cruisers in making captures; the impartiality of national prize tribunals, the number of prizes and the number of condemnations made in a particular war; questions of vital interest to both belligerent and neutral merchantmen plying their trade on the high seas in time of war.

It is the purpose of this paper to investigate the character of prize money laws in force in various countries at different periods of their history, the conditions which have given rise to such rules, and the effect particular rules have had upon maritime captures in time of war.

CHAPTER I. AMONG THE ANCIENTS.

PART 1. GREECE.

a. Land War.

The Greeks are possibly the earliest people who attained a sufficient degree of civilization to have any definite laws of war, consequently we shall first look to them for laws of prize distribution. In his chapter on "the right of acquiring things captured in war", Grotius treats at length the condition of private property in war among the ancients. His remarks are intended to refer to both land and naval warfare though in fact all his instances are drawn from land warfare. It is probable that the same theories applied in both cases though on the high seas from the nature of the case, the state would have much greater difficulty in enforcing any restrictions upon the right of making captures and appropriating the profits therefrom than on land.

In regard to the Greek treatment of prize, Grotius says:

"After the battle of Plataea there was a severe edict that no one should privately take any part of the booty. Afterwards when Athens was conquered the booty was made public property by Lysander and the Spartan officers who had to deal with the measure were called prize sellers. If we go to Asia the Trojans were accustomed as Virgil teaches to draw prize lots as is done in dividing common property. In other cases the decision of the matter was with the general and by this right Hector promises Dolon the horses of Achilles when he stipulates for them, by which you may see that the right of prize treasure was not in the captor alone. So when Cyrus was victor, the booty was taken to him, and when Alexander, to him."

In his work on International law among the ancients, Phillipson has presented similar instances of the distribution of booty. He adds to the statement made by Grotius in regard to the battle of Plataea that after making proclamation that no one should take the booty "Pausanias ordered the helots to collect the treasure of which one tithe was allotted to the Gods at Delphi, another to the Olympian God, and a third to the God at the Isthmus, and the rest was divided according to title and merit. An additional reward was also given to those who particularly distinguished themselves, and a special portion reserved for Pausanias." and again, "In 426 B.C. when Ambracia was reduced by the Acaranians with the help of the Athenians under Demosthenes, a third part of the spoils was assigned to Athens, three hundred panoplies to Demosthenes and the remainder divided by the Acaranians among their cities."

Similar practices have been noted by Prof. Amos S. Hershey in a recent article. He says "It was customary to divide the booty amongst the victorious soldiery, i.e. after devoting one tenth of the spoil to the Gods and a portion to the leaders and warriors who had particularly distinguished themselves."

The Greeks also appear to have recognized the right of reprisal. Thus in the Iliad, Nestor speaks of making reprisals on the Epeian nation, in satisfaction for a prize won by his father Neleus at the Elian games and for debts due to many private subjects of the Pylian kingdom. The booty was equitably divided among the many creditors.

This testimony is based on the writings of Herodotus, Plutarch, Xenophon, Homer, Virgil, Pliny and other classical writers. It has little bearing on our present subject except in so far as it indicates the recognition even at so early an age of the principle that the title to captured property does not rest in the immediate captor but that proceeds of prize shall be equitably divided by the general or other officer. In the case of the battle of Plataea there seems to be also a recognition of the principle that prizes of right belong to the whole public, in other words to the state.

These two principles, that prizes do not belong to the original captor but should be divided, and that the state may appropriate prizes seem to constitute the Greek theory on the subject. It is unlikely that they were the subject of definite laws but recognition was given to them if at all by command of the general on the occasion of a particular war, as is indicated in the cases cited.

The basis for this theory, apparently far ahead of its time may be found in the well developed feeling of political obligation among the Greeks. They appear to have recognized public war as a state affair, consequently individual soldiers acted only in the capacity of agents of the state in regular military operations. Their captures accrued not to themselves but to the state for whom they acted.

Of the actual effect of such a prize law among the Greeks it is difficult to make a statement. It might be supposed that the incentive toward the capture of booty would be decreased by such a rule yet so far as we can learn of Greek warfare there was no limit to the atrocities committed either on persons or property. The Greek soldier felt justified in going to any extreme in acting for his state.

b. Maritime War.

Grotius has nothing to say of prize laws in maritime warfare. Phillipson believes that the Greeks made prize of enemy vessels and also of neutral vessels for breach of blockade. He gives evidence which indicates that theoretically, confiscable goods went to the state, and that rudimentary prize courts were held. Thus he says:

"In most Greek states there was something of the nature of a prize court, to which appeals could be made by those who held they had been contrary to the law of nations deprived of their property. In Athens, the assembly of the people frequently took cognizance of such claims. Thus two trierarchs were accused of appropriating the proceeds of a cargo from Naucrates on the ground that if confiscable it ought to have gone to the State. An assembly was therefore held and the people voted for a hearing on the question." But in general, law at sea was very poorly enforced and neutral rights seldom respected. In fact it seems likely that maritime war fell little short of piracy so far as the capture of private property was concerned. Thus Polycrates of Samos wishing to establish his supremacy on the Aegean built up a navy which swept the sea, robbing friend and foe alike, and so "at the commencement of the Peloponnesian war the Lacedaemonians captured not only the trading vessels of their enemy the Athenians, and also of their allies, but even those of neutral states and all who were taken on board were treated as enemies and indiscriminately slaughtered."

The Aegean sea was a nest of pirates and the profession was looked upon not only as a legitimate means of emolument but was even considered glorious. They were frequently engaged in war as mercenaries. Thus Psammilicha was reinforced by Carian and Ionian pirates, Euripidas and Aelotian employed pirates as mercenaries in 218 B.C. and Polyxenidas the commander of the fleet of Antiocha entered into an alliance with Nicander, a pirate chief who contributed five decked ships in 190 B.C. In such cases of course the state surrendered all right in controlling the distribution of prize money or of itself sharing in the proceeds.

The Rhodian sea laws are said to have been effective in the third century B.C. in temporarily freeing the sea of Pirates and giving opportunity for considerable commercial advancement. Unfortunately these laws have been almost entirely lost so we do not know what measures were taken for disposing of the captured pirate vessels or other enemy goods that might be considered prize.

It seems that the theory of the states control over prize applied in naval as in land war but that in practice government authority at no period of ancient Greek history extended very effectively over the seas for any considerable length of time and that private property was for the most part at the tender mercies of the pirates.

NOTES.

Chapter I, Part 1.

Grotius, Hugo. De Jure Belli et Pacis. 3 Vols. Original and English translation from the Latin by William Whewell. Cambridge, England, lib. iii, c vi, p. 104.

Op. cit. iii, 123.

Heroditus, ix, 79, quoted in Grotius, op. cit. iii, 123.

Plutarch, Lysander, 442 a, quoted ibid.

Xenophon, de Lacedemonia Republica, c 13, n 11, quoted ibid.

Virgil, Aeneid, ix, 268, quoted ibid.

Homer, Iliad, v, 331, quoted ibid.

Euripides, Rhes. v, 182, quoted ibid.

Pliny, xxxiii, 3, quoted ibid.

Coleman Phillipson. The International Law and Custom of Ancient Greece and Rome. 2 Vols. London, 1911.

Heroditus, ix, 80, 81, quoted in Phillipson, op. cit. ii, 237.

Thucidides, iii, 114; Heroditus, viii, 11, 123; Plutarch, Alcibiades, 7; Plato, Synp. 220; quoted in Plato op. cit. ii, 237.

Hershey, Amos S. The History of International Relations During Antiquity and the Middle Ages. American Journal of International Law, 1911, v. 915.

Homer, Iliad, lib ii, quoted in Blackstone, Commentaries, i, 259.

Fustel de Coulanges, The Ancient City, English Translation from French by Willard Small, 10th Edition, Boston, 1901, p. 293.

Wheaton, History of the Law of Nations, New York, 1845, p. 5. Walker, History of the Law of Nations, Cambridge, Eng., 1899, p. 41.

"To a king or commander nothing is unjust which is useful." Thucydides, History, lib vi, quoted in Wheaton, History, p. 5; see also Hershey, op. cit. American Journal of International Law, v. 915.

Phillipson, op. cit. ii, 381.

Walker, History, p. 41. Walker, Science of International Law, Cambridge, England, 1893, p. 60.

G. W. Botsford, A History of Greece, New York, 1912, p. 75.

Thucydides, ii, 67, quoted in Phillipson, op. cit. ii, 382.

Homer, Iliad, i, 367; vi, 58; ix, 588, xxii. 64; Odyssey, xv, 385; 426; xvii, 425; quoted in Phillipson, op. cit. 370.

Heroditus, ii, 152, quoted in Phillipson, op. cit. ii, 371.

Polybius, iv, 68, quoted ibid.

Livy, xxxvii, 11, quoted ibid.

The so-called Rhodian laws of the middle ages, the earliest manuscript of which apparently dates from 1478, have no connection with the ancient sea laws of Rhodes. Of the latter only the law of Jettison survives, see Robert D. Benedict, The Historical Position of the Rhodian Law, Yale Law Journal, 1908-09, xviii, 223; Hershey, op. cit. Amer. Jour. of International Law, 1911, v. 917; Walter Ashburner, the Rhodian Sea Law, Oxford, 1909.

Hershey, op. cit. American Journal of International Law, 1911, v. 915; Phillipson, op. cit. ii, 373.

PART 2. ROME.

a. Land War.

From the Greek theories the Roman legal mind developed elaborate rules for the apportionment of booty captured in land war. The Romans clearly recognized that the prizes taken in public war belong to the state.

"Whatever is captured from the enemy, the law directs to be public property: so that not only private persons are not the owners of it, but even the general is not. The Questor takes it, sells it and carries the money to the public account." says Dionysius of Halicarnassus. This might seem to imply that no individual could enjoy a share of the proceeds but such does not seem to have been the case. It simply means that the title to all captures vested in the state which could if it saw fit transfer a share of the booty to the captors or others. Grotius gives definite rules employed by the Romans in dividing the produce of such booty. His statements are based on the writings of Livy and other Latin writers.

In dividing booty money account was taken of the pay of the soldiers and of special bravery. Special reward was usually made to the general. Sometimes a portion was given to others who had contributed to the expenses of the war. Often a portion was dedicated to the Gods although this practice was much less common among them than among the Greeks. It was considered a particularly worthy act on the part of a general if he refused to accept any share of the booty as was sometimes done by those seeking state honors. The whole system was closely circumscribed by law. A penalty attached to the crime of peculation, the private secreting of booty without submitting it to the public. Roman orators dilated at length on the infamy of peculation.

These rules applied only to soldiers of the regular army engaged in regular war. In irregular warfare soldiers were often given the privilege of committing indiscriminate pillage in which case the booty belonged to the captor. This practice however was greatly deplored by many writers. Captures made by allies not under the immediate commands of Roman generals or by subjects carrying on war without pay at their own risk accrued to the sole benefit of the captors.

b. Maritime War.

As to captures at sea, the Jurisconsult Valneius Maecianus said, "I am master of the earth, but the law is mistress of the sea." Grotius has nothing to say directly of maritime captures among the Romans, though he implies that the same laws applied to them as to land captures. A case of naval prize arose during the Punic war in the capture of the Carthaginian woman, Saphonoba, from a vessel at sea. The Roman general considered that all prize of war belonged to the Roman people and was to be divided by the senate, so ordered that she be sent to Rome. The lady settled the matter by taking poison.

The Romans were a land people. They very much disliked naval warfare, consequently they never supported much of a fleet. True, on meeting a naval power like Carthage they created a very effective navy on short notice but whenever they could they avoided naval warfare. Piracy was extremely prevalent on the Mediterranean during Roman times. Often Roman generals made use of pirate vessels both for transport and to harass the enemy. In these cases of course the state put up no claim to control prizes. Later, pirates became so powerful that Rome saw the necessity of crushing them. Servilius actively engaged in suppressing piracy and he felt bound to render full account to Rome of all captures. Pompey finally crushed the pirates in the battle of Coracesum B.C. 67 and completely drove them out of the Mediterranean. The Romans recognized the right of reprisal and according to Chancellor Kent they required the carriage of a commission by vessels engaged in that business.

Roman law, then, recognized that captures were the property of the state, that apportionment should be governed by law, that in special cases the state could waive all right in favor of the immediate captors.

Rome's policy was directed toward the securing of order through law. Discipline and authority were the fundamental principles on which her greatness was founded. Her military policy was to subordinate individuals to the general good, to make each soldier a cog in the wheel working in harmony with the whole. Individual freedom of action was curtailed not in the interests of humanity but in the interests of the efficiency of the general army. Her rules of prize distribution are completely in harmony with these principles. No private right of aggrandizement in war existed, all was controlled by the state. The state was the combatant in war, the state bore the losses and to the state accrued the gains. State authority overshadowed every act of the individual.

In practical effects the Roman laws of prize money probably accomplished the purpose for which they were intended, that is, they lessened the chance for insubordination among the soldiers. Under them soldiers remained at their post of duty instead of going on journeys of pillage. It made war regular and public instead of guerrilla and private.

Humanitarian effects were slight or none at all. Though not impelled by the hope of personal gain the Roman soldiers seem to have captured, devastated and destroyed without compunction. Wheaton says of Roman warfare, "Victory made even the sacred things of the enemy profane, confiscated all his property, moveable and immoveable, public and private, doomed him and his posterity to perpetual slavery and dragged his kings and generals at the chariot wheels of the conqueror thus depressing an enemy in his spirit and pride of mind, the only consolation he has left when his strength and power are annihilated."

Though Roman warfare was cruel, it was regulated by law. Roman civilization recognized the supremacy of the state, the public character of regular war, and of immediate interest to the present subject, the exclusive control by the state of all military captures.

NOTES.

Chapter I, Part 2.

Antiquita Roma, vii, 63, quoted in Grotius, op. cit. iii, 124.

Grotius, op. cit. iii, 127.

Livy, xiv, 34, 40, 43, quoted in Grotius, op. cit. iii, 129.

Heroditus, ix, 80, quoted in Grotius, op. cit. iii, 130.

Dionysius of Halicarnassus, v, 47, quoted, in Grotius, op. cit. iii, 134.

Livy, v, 23, quoted in Grotius, op. cit. iii, 135; Phillipson, op. cit. ii, 238.

Apud Dionysius of Halicarnassus Excerpt, p. 714, quoted in Grotius, op. cit. iii, 131.

Polybius, History, x, 16, quoted in Grotius, op. cit. iii, 138.

Cato, xi, 18; Cicero, Verres, iv, 41, quoted in Grotius, op. cit. iii, 137, 138.

Livy, xliv, 45; xlv, 34, quoted in Grotius, op. cit. iii, 133.

Livy, v, 20, quoted in Grotius, op. cit. iii, 134.

Cald. Cons. 85, quoted in Grotius, op. cit. iii, 140.

Digest, xiv, 3, quoted in Charles Calvo, Le Droit International Theorique et Pratique, 5th Edition, 6 Vols., Paris, 1896, i, 15.

Livy, xxx, 14; 11 Appian Pun. 28, quoted in W. E. Heitland, The Roman Republic, 3 Vols., Cambridge, England, 1909, sec. 385.

Heitland, op. cit. secs. 246, 436; Phillipson, op. cit. ii, 369.

Heitland, op. cit. sec. 161.

Heitland, op. cit. sec. 245.

Heitland, op. cit. secs. 949, 960.

Cicero, Verres, i, 56, 57, quoted in Heitland, op. cit. sec. 965.

Heitland, op. cit. sec. 993.

Kent, Commentaries, Holmes, Editor, 12th Edition, 4 Vols., Boston, 1893, i, 95.

de Coulanges, op. cit. 293.

Wheaton, History of the Law of Nations, p. 25.

CHAPTER II. DURING THE MIDDLE AGES.

PART 1. MARITIME CODES.

"In the dark ages, between 476 and 800 A.D. International law reached its nadir in the West". Private war, on land and piracy at sea were unrestrained. There were of course no laws providing for the division of prize money.

By the eleventh and twelfth centuries many cities of the Mediterranean and North seas had become powerful commercially and issued laws for determining maritime affairs. Such were the Amalfitan Tables, the Judgments or Roles of Oleron, the Laws of Wisby, and the Consolato del Mare originating in Barcelona. As these laws simply stated the universal customs of the sea it came about that all maritime towns would adopt one of these codes. Thus by the fifteenth century the Consolato del Mare was recognized maritime law in most of the commercial cities of the Mediterranean while the Judgments of Oleron were in a similar way recognized by the towns of the North Sea. These laws were intended primarily to regulate the private relations of mariners, owners and merchants, but on account of the necessity of protection from pirates many of them also included laws of maritime war and prize. State organization had not developed sufficiently to afford protection to merchants on the sea, consequently the merchants themselves formed protective organizations, furnished armed cruisers for making prizes and established consulates for judging maritime cases and for enforcing the definite codes of maritime law.

The Consolato Del Mare may be taken as an example of the maritime codes. It probably originated in the thirteenth century. The earliest known manuscripts are in the Catalonian language and apparently were engrossed in the middle of the fourteenth century. The earliest printed copy is dated 1494 and is also in the Catalonian language. The chapters on prize law, state the principles on which enemy property may be captured. In general the principle is established that enemy vessels and neutral goods are exempt. Originally the armed merchantmen were in no way bound to any state so no commission delegating state authority to make captures is mentioned. Apparently the prizes had to be adjudicated at the consulates established by the merchant leagues.

There are chapters dealing with "cruizers" which give the municipal usages concerning the distribution of prize between the owners, officers and crew of vessels.

"Thus among the Italians a third part of a captured ship goes to the captain of the victorious ship, a third part to the merchants to whom the cargo belonged, and a third part to the sailors".

It thus appears that the Consolato distinctly recognized the reign of law in prize matters. It respected neutral rights, it required adjudication on prizes, it gave rules for the division of prize money, respecting the claims of merchants, captain and crew to share in the distribution.

The rules of the Consolato appeal to one decidedly as rules intended to govern commercial enterprises. The policy of the merchants was of defensive rather than offensive war so no stringent belligerent rights were affirmed. Primarily intended for commerce, it is not surprising that such a large amount of respect was paid to neutral rights and such a large share of the prizes given to merchants. The minute rules, seemingly forecasting every possible contingency also speak of a strong desire to establish order, and firm law, both conditions essential to commerce.

The Consolato was probably effective for its purpose. We know that the merchant guilds and the maritime towns flourished, piracy decreased, commerce prospered. The merchant sailors would not be likely to be lured into making prizes for private gain when their very object was the destruction of piracy. Also habits of commerce and obedience to law would induce them to exhibit moderation in war matters. The maritime laws and the supremacy of the commercial towns was a great step toward legalizing maritime warfare and especially toward ameliorating the condition of private property on the sea.

One of the peculiarities of the Consolato from a modern standpoint is that it does not recognize the exclusive right of states to make war. This is explained by the fact that territorial states had not become sufficiently centralized to organize a definite maritime jurisdiction. However, in the early part of the sixteenth century the movement toward the individualizing of territorial states was rapidly nearing completion and it is interesting to note that when the movement was sufficiently advanced nearly all the states adopted one of the old maritime codes into their laws, of course adding to it the principle of state authorization for all reprisals or wars and state jurisdiction over prize cases.

NOTES.

Chapter II, Part 1.

Walker, History of the Law of Nations, p. 64.

For brief discussion of many of the Maritime Codes see E. C. Benedict, The American Admiralty, 4th Edition, Albany, 1910. The so-called Rhodian Sea Laws are thought by Ashburner to date from the seventh or eighth century A. D. Other writers place them later. The earliest manuscript apparently dates from the fifteenth century. It is well established that they have no connection with the ancient sea laws of Rhodes but possibly they were authorized by the Byzantine Caesars and undoubtedly they consist of laws recognized in the Eastern Mediterranean in the middle ages. These laws relate only to civil matters at sea and have no provisions dealing with prize but in their general provisions they may have furnished a basis for the maritime codes of a few centuries later, see Ashburner, The Rhodian Sea Law, Oxford, 1909.

Twiss, Introduction to the "Black Book of the Admiralty", Rolls Series, No. 55, iii, 80.

For discussion of the influence of the Consolato, see Twiss, Consulate of the Sea, Encyclopedia Britannica, 11th Edition, vii, 23. Ashburner takes a less favorable view of the Consolato. He considers it a literary production giving the authors theory of sea law rather than a correct statement of the law as it was. In his opinion more confidence should be placed in the maritime statutes of the towns such as the laws of Amalaric, St. Cuzala, Genoa, St. Ancon, Baracchi, St. Caltaro, etc. than in the Consolato.— Ashburner, op. cit. p. 120.

For discussion of the Laws of Oleron, see Twiss, Sea Laws, Encyclopedia Britannica, 11th Edition, xxiii, 535; Sir John Comyn, A Digest of the Laws of England, 5 Vols., Dublin, 1785, i, 271; also note post p. 42.

Wheaton, History of the Law of Nations, p. 62.

For discussion of origin and early manuscripts see Twiss, Introduction to "The Black Book of the Admiralty", iii, 26 et seq.

For text of prize chapters of the Consolato, see English translation by Dr. Robinson in his Collectanea Maritima, No. v; quoted in Wheaton, History of the Law of Nations, p. 63; Original and translation by Twiss, Black Book of the Admiralty, Rolls Series No. 55, iii, 539; French translation by Pardessus, in his Collection des Lois Maritimes Anterieures aux XVIII Siecle, ii, c 12, noted in Wheaton, op. cit. p. 61, Walker, History of the Law of Nations, p. 116; See also note by Grotius, op. cit. iii, 9.

Twiss, Introduction to Black Book of the Admiralty, iii, 76.

Consolato Del Mare, c 285, quoted in Grotius op. cit. iii, 145.

Wheaton, History of the Law of Nations, p. 66.

PART 2. THE NEW INTERNATIONAL LAW.

During the sixteenth century the idea of the individuality of territorial states reached material realization. A school of international law writers arose who endeavored to determine the relations which ought to exist between these states. A new recognition was given to the state's exclusive authority over matters of war and prize. The old Roman laws of JusGentium and JusNaturale were combined with the observed practices of nations to build up rules conformable to the new situation.

Machiavelli writing in 1513 distinctly recognized the independence of the territorial state. He conceived of the Prince as being under obligations to no superior, either human or divine. He recognized the state as the sole agency which could authorize war and the capture of prize but recommended liberality in distributing the produce of prize and booty as a policy calculated to encourage loyalty and perseverance in the soldiers, a theory well in harmony with his idea of human nature, which considered man as actuated solely by the hope of personal gain.

Conrad Brunus in 1548 also voiced the theory of state supremacy in war. "The war making power resides in the supreme authority of the state to whom it exclusively belongs to authorize hostilities against other nations by a solemn declaration."

Francis de Victoria held that captured moveables become by the law of nations property of the captors but pillage should be only permitted when necessary for reducing the enemy.

Balthazar Ayala took an even more advanced stand. He pointed out that according to the laws of Spain, lands, houses and ships of war taken from the enemy become the property of the crown and as to other articles the right of the captors to appropriate them as booty is restrained by that of the state to regulate the division reserving to itself a certain share and distributing the rest according to the respective rank of the captors. In regard to naval captures he says:

"But if it chance that in naval war the king supplies the ships and their armament and also provides supplies and wages for the soldiers and sailors the same contributions place the whole booty at the disposal not of the general or admiral but of the king, nor will the soldiers or sailors get any part thereof except such as is granted to them by the king's liberality. In every other event however, after the king's share has been set aside, the admiral can divide the residue between the soldiers and sailors a seventh part of the residue being due to himself". Ayala had previously remarked that by the Spanish law the king's share ranged from one fifth to one half of the prize. In his theory goods must be brought within the territory of the capturing state (intra praesidia) to give a good title. If recaptured before this, by postliminium, they revert to the original owner. Reprisals must be authorized by the sovereign.

Thomas More conceived of a liberal policy of disposing of prize, in his Utopia. In speaking of the capture of cities he says, "If they knowe that annye cytezeins counselled to yealde and rendre vp the citie, to them they gyue parts of the condemned mens goods. They resydewe they distribute and giue frelye amonge them, whose helpe they had in the same warre. For none of themselfes taketh any portion of the praye."

Bodin clearly enunciated the sovereigns exclusive right over sea captures. "Mais les droits de la mer n'appartiennent qu'au Prince Souverain."

Gentilis the forerunner of Grotius expressed the limitations on the power of the state. There was danger that in the rise of states to independence the Machiavellian policy would be adopted, that states would consider themselves bound by no law. Gentilis showed the limitations that natural law impose upon states even in war. In his view, property can not be wantonly destroyed, neutral property can never be captured and neutral territory is always inviolable.

In his epoch making work which appeared in 1625, Grotius correlates the principles of those preceding him and in authoritative style sets forth the new international law. His chapters on prize distribution may be briefly summarized as follows: The right of reprisal is recognized but it is only allowable under authority of the state. In the case of reprisals the property in goods taken immediately accrues to the captor to the extent of the debt or damages due and expenses, but any balance over this ought to be restored. The prize should be adjudged in a court of the state before distribution. Goods captured at sea require firm possession to give a title. In Roman law this is established when the vessel is brought to port (intra praesidia), but modern practice establishes the twenty four hour rule. Recaptures, before possession is established, revert to the original owner by postliminium. Neutral property is never subject to capture not even in enemy ships. Enemy property is good prize. If taken otherwise than in regular public service, i.e. in private reprisals, or under special grant of pillage, it becomes the property of the immediate captor though the municipal law of the captors state may alter this condition. Goods taken in public service accrue to the state which may distribute the proceeds at will. Instances are given of the distribution laws in contemporary states. "Among the Italians a third part of a captured ship goes to the captain of the victorious ship, a third part to the merchants to whom the cargo belonged and a third part to the sailors." "With the Spaniards, if ships are sent out at private expense, part of the prize goes to the king, part to the high admiral, and ships of war go altogether to the king." By the custom of France, the Admiral has a tenth, and so with the Hollanders but here a fifth part of the booty is taken by the state.

Zouche of Oxford University, England, in 1650 made a valuable contribution to international law literature in his "Juris et Judicii Fecialis sive Juris Inter gentes Explicatia", a book famed as being the first to describe the science as jus inter gentes, international law, rather than the former misleading name, jus gentium, law of nations. He maintains that war can only be declared by the supreme authority of the state. However if acts of aggression are committed by individuals during war without authorization, international law has no jurisdiction over the matter, though municipal law may decree punishment. As coming from England this theory is interesting as it seems to forecast the later doctrine of that country that unauthorized captures at sea are permissible so far as the enemy is concerned though municipal law decrees the whole product of such captures to the crown. Zouche admits the right of reprisal. By reprisal is understood the right assumed by a subject to collect a foreign debt or to collect damages for injuries received in a foreign country through the seizure of goods on the high seas belonging to any subject of that state. Though the practice seems hard to reconcile with justice, Zouche in common with most of the international law writers holds that all the members of a state are liable for the debts of one member so by strict international law, reprisal is allowable but only under commission from the sovereign.

Puffendorf writing in 1672 practically quotes the views of Grotius in prize matters. He maintains that individuals can not make war, which is only a state affair, "Il est certain, que c'est au souverain seul qu'appartient le droit de faire la guerre." In regard to captures he holds that the title to booty vests originally in the sovereign but it is equitable for the sovereign to divide the proceeds among those who have borne the heaviest burdens of war. Recaptures revert to the original owner. The right of reprisals is admitted but exception is taken to the view of Grotius that in case of reprisals and all captures made by private undertaking the proceeds belong immediately to the captor. Puffendorf asserts "Tout le droit que les particuliers ant ici depend toujours originairement de la volonte du souverain," thus emphasizing more strongly the absolute title of the state to all captures. A careful reading of Grotius seems to reveal that his idea was the same. He says that by the practice of nations captures not made in regular war usually accrue to the captor but this rule may be changed by municipal law and "so a rule may be introduced by law that all things which are taken from the enemy shall be public property," thus virtually asserting Puffendorf's statement that the original title always vests in the sovereign.

In brief the laws of prize distribution enunciated by the great founders of international law of the sixteenth and seventeenth centuries appear to be as follows:

1. The state is the only power which can prosecute war and make prize.

2. The right of private reprisal can only be exercised under specific commission from the state.

3. The title to all prizes vests originally in the state.

4. Distribution should be decreed only after adjudication of the prize by a regular tribunal of the state.

5. The method of distributing prize money is determined by municipal law.

Undoubtedly the practice of nations did not, in a great many cases equal the lofty ideals of the publicists but at the same time their principles were for the most part given theoretic recognition by the sovereign authorities of states belonging to the family of nations and as centralized authority gained in strength they became more and more realized in practice.

NOTES.

Chapter II, Part 2.

"The Prince" was written in 1513, first published 1532, posthumously.

"Princes ought avoid as much as they are able to stand in anothers discretion." Machiavelli, The Prince, English Translation from Italian by Dacres, Tudor Translations, vol. 39, London, 1905, c 21.

"And therefore it suffices to conceive this, that a Prince, and especially a new Prince can not observe all those things for which men are held good, he being often forced for the maintenance of his state to do contrary to his faith, charity, humanity, and religion."—The Prince, c 18, p. 323. "And therefore, a wise Prince can not, nor ought not keep his faith given, when the observance thereof turns to disadvantage and the occasions that made him promise are past." The Prince, c 18, p. 322.

"The Prince" c 16, p. 315.

For Machiavelli's political theory see W. A. Dunning, A History of Political Theories, 2 Vols, New York, 1902, i, 285 et seq.

De Legationibus, 1548, iii, 8, quoted in Wheaton, History of the Law of Nations, p. 50.

Reflectiones Theologicae, 1557, vi, 52, quoted in Wheaton, op. cit. p. 41; Walker, History of the Law of Nations, p. 229.

De Jure et Officiis Bellicis et Disciplina Militari, 1582, Original and English translation from Latin by J. P. Bate, J. Westlake, Editor, 2 Vols, Carnegie Institution of Washington, 1912, ii, 38; taken from Spanish Ordinance, Book 14, tit. 26, par. 2.

Op. cit. Lib. i, c 4, 5, also see Wheaton, op. cit. p. 45 Walker, op. cit. p. 248.

Utopia, 1516, English translation from Latin by Robynson, Arber, Editor, English Reprint Series, vol. 2, London, 1869, p. 142, also quoted in Walker, op. cit. p. 242.

De La Republique, 1577, Liv. i, c 10, p. 246, quoted in Walker, op. cit. p. 262.

De Jure Belli, 1589, Holland Editor, Oxford, 1877, p. 250, see also Walker, op. cit. p. 265.

De Jure Belli et Pacis, 1625, Edition Cited, see also summary by Walker, op. cit. 313 et seq.

Op. cit. iii, 48.

Op. cit. iii. 111.

Op. cit. iii, 105.

Op. cit. iii, 145, taken from Consolato Del Mare, c 285.

Op. cit. iii, 145, taken from Leg. Hisp. xix, tit. xxvi, p. 2, 1.

Op. cit. iii, 144, taken from Leg. Hisp. iv, tit. xxvi, p. 2.

Op. cit. iii, 145, taken from Const. Gall. liv. xx, tit. 14, art. 1.

Op. cit. iii, 145.

Juris et Judicii Fecialis sive Juris Inter Gentes Explicatio, 1650 original and English translation from Latin by J. L. Brierly, T. E. Holland, Editor, 2 Vols., Carnegie Institution of Washington, 1911, ii. 112.

Post 81, 103.

Op. cit. ii, 115.

Le Droit de la Nature et des Gens, French translation by Barbeyrac, 2 Vols., Leide, 1759, ii, liv. viii, c 6, s 8, p. 558 et seq.

Op. cit. ii, 569.

Op. cit. ii, 570.

De Jure Belli et Pacis, Edition cited, ii, 122.

CHAPTER III. GREAT BRITAIN, HISTORICAL RESUME.

PART 1. EARLIEST TIMES TO 1340.

a. Laws.

The practice of Great Britain in prize distribution has always been remarkable for its extreme liberality to the captors of prize. Chancellor Kent has a note to the effect that by common law "goods taken from an enemy belong to the captor." His authority is a case decided in King's Bench in 1697 which says, "And it was resolved by whole court that though, if goods be taken from an enemy it vests the property in the party taking them, by our (common) law, yet by admiralty law, the property of a ship taken without letters of mart vests in the king upon the taking, and this on the high seas." The same view is expressed by a modern writer, who says, "The root of the prize system is found in the ancient doctrine that any person might seize to his own use, goods belonging to an alien enemy and this right extended to captures at sea."

A case in the reign of Edward III, 1343, bears out these opinions. The king of Aragon complained of a case of piracy by Englishmen and asked redress. Edward called his Chancellor and council and the decision was given that the alleged piracy was a case of lawful prize and that by the law maritime the goods belonged to the captor.

However, England very early recognized the contrary principle that prize of war of right belongs to the state and private individuals only acquire their title by grant of the crown or parliament. Thus by a patent of 1242, Henry III granted half of all prizes taken by them to masters and crews of king's ships and the same to the men of Oleron and Bayonne in their own ships. In 1295 a letter patent provided that the whole of prizes taken by Bayonne ships should be shared equally between the owners and men and in the Scotch expedition of 1319 Edward II also granted the whole of prizes to the captors.

A close Roll of 1325 states that men of the Cinque Ports had granted one fourth of all prizes to the king. The Portsmen by a grant of William the Conqueror enjoyed special privileges in prize matters and claimed to enjoy prizes of their own right. In early times their forces comprised the greater part of England's naval strength so this privilege was quite important. However, the kings seem to have wished to regain some of the jurisdiction which they had granted away and in the case mentioned Edward II tried to gain jurisdiction over the whole of the prize. In 1326 the king's primal right seemed to be recognized as superior to that of the Portsmen for a grant of that date is made by the king, of all prizes to the portsmen.

b. Administration.

During this period no machinery for adjudication was established. The only means through which the king could collect a share of prize was through the common law courts and they proved in most cases inadequate. The jealously guarded jurisdictions of the Cinque ports also largely interfered with the king's perquisites in prize. Their peculiar customs were held above the king's right. Thus in 1293 when Edward I claimed a share of prizes captured by Portsmen they stated that on the occasion in question they had hoisted a flag called the "Baucon". This action meant a fight to the death in which case by the universally recognized law of the sea all prizes captured by the survivors belonged to them. Furthermore if the king endeavored to interfere with them they would leave the country. Such assertions of independence probably prevented much state interference with prize distribution at this period.

NOTES.

Chapter III, Part 1.

Kent, Commentaries on International law, Abdy edition, Cambridge, 1866, p. 271.

King vs. Broom, 12 Mod. 135; 88 English Reports 1217.

H. E. Smith, Studies in Juridical Law, Chicago, 1902, p. 139.

R. G. Marsdon, introduction to select pleas of the Admiralty, Seldon Series, vi.

Rymer, Foedera, 20 Vols., London, 1704-1735, i, 408.

Calendar of Patent Rolls, Ed. I, 1292-1301, m 16, p. 130.

R. G. Marsdon, Early Prize Jurisdiction in England, English Historical Review, xxiv, 675.

Calendar of Close Rolls, Ed. II, 1323-1327, m 26, p. 412.

D. J. Medley, A Student's Manual of English Constitutional History, Oxford, 1907, p. 485.

Rymer, op. cit. iv, 226.

Marsdon, English Historical Review, xxiv, 677.

PART 2. 1340-1485.

a. Laws.

After the battle of Sluys in 1340 when Edward III became in fact master of the seas, a title which kings of England had assumed since the time of John, the king issued certain ordinances for the distribution of prize. A distinction was made between prizes taken by ships in the king's pay and privateers. At that time there was no navy owned by the state. In the former case the king is to receive one fourth of the proceeds of all prizes, the owner of the vessel one fourth and the remainder "shall belong to those who took them which halfe ought to be shared equally between them". Out of the portion going to the captors the admiral has two shares or as much as two mariners from each ship, if he is present when the capture is made, if absent he only receives one share. It is also provided that "ships out of sight shall receive no share unless sailing toward and in sight so as to help the takers if need be." The apparent purport of this anomalous language being that joint captors must be of actual constructive assistance to share. In the case of privateers the king has no share of prizes. The whole amount goes to the captors except the admirals perquisite which is the same as in the former case. It is further provided that "whoever takes a ship ought to bring it before the admiral, there to take and receive what the law and custom of the sea requires", no plunder of the prize being permitted before adjudication except on the decks.

By a patent of 1386 the king gives all his share to the admiral and in the following year the whole of prizes is granted to privateers.

In 1406 a grant of Henry IV provides that ship owners shall have prizes taken from the enemy but they must deliver up to the king any prisoners they may take for whom a reasonable reward will be given. In the same year a letter from the admiral calls on all mariners to enter the king's service and says that "whatever profits and gains such persons shall make from the king's enemies on said voyages they shall have and enjoy freely without impediment or disturbance." By statute of 1416 it was provided that letters of Marque might be issued by the privy council to any one having grievances against a foreign power. In such issues of letters of Marque the profit of goods taken went to the captor to the extent of the damages received. All goods in excess of that amount were supposed to be returned but few cases of such return are on record. It was under authority of this act that letters of Marque were issued in England until the final abolition of the practice in the treaty of Paris of 1856.

A treaty with Flanders of 1426 contains the provision that "no prizes shall be divided at sea or in a foreign harbour but shall be brought entire to a port of England and there it will be adjudged by the king and council, the chancellor or the admiral whether the prize belonged to friends or enemies and it will be disposed of in good and brief manner." Here we seem to have a distinct enunciation of the most modern principles of prize law that no title to prize is legally conferred until after adjudication by a competent organ of the state making the capture.

In 1442 an ordinance of Henry VI "for the safeguarding of the sea" emphasizes these same principles. It declares that neutrals must not be harmed in war and that award of prize must be made by a competent tribunal before distribution of proceeds. The scheme to be used in distributing the proceeds in case the vessel is found good prize is as follows: One half goes to the master, quarter master, sailors and soldiers. The remainder is to be divided into three parts, of which two go to the owners and one to the chief and under captains. The ordinance also contains rules for the conduct of privateers. In the same year a statute permitted any one making capture of an enemy vessel "to take the goods and merchandises and enjoy them without any restitution thereof to be made in any wise, even though the goods belonged to neutrals and they had no safe conduct from the king of England."

Shortly before this, the collection of sea laws known as the Black book of the Admiralty was compiled for the use of the Lord High Admiral. The book contains that ancient body of sea law, the Roles of Oleron, besides several later ordinances and inquests. The principle portion dealing with prize distribution is part "A" which consists of the ordinance of Edward III made after the battle of Sluys, already mentioned. It also contains "An inquisition made at Queensborough in 1375" which is a statement by a jury of the existing law at that time. It restates the earlier ordinance of Edward III except that the king's share of prizes is not mentioned. The inquest also permits merchant ships to make captures from the king's enemies, apparently without a special commission and divide the proceeds two thirds to the owner and one third to the mariners. Captures by merchant vessels without commission seem to have been quite common and were openly approved by the king. The fact that these ancient ordinances were collected for authoritative use seems to indicate that they were recognized law in the fifteenth century.

b. Administration.

The period of the hundred years war, thus brought about definite progress in prize money laws. Prize distribution became the subject of definite ordinances. In Edward Third's ordinance most of the principles of prize distribution mentioned by international law writers of three centuries later were enunciated. The issuance of such an ordinance implied a recognition of the principle, "bello parta cedunt reipublicae" the original title to prize vests in the state. Definite rules for distribution were declared and most important of all, adjudication of prizes by a competent court was demanded before distribution. The office of admiral was created by Edward I in the year 1300 when Gervase Alvard was appointed Admiral of the Cinque Ports. At first several admirals were appointed with jurisdiction over different portions of the sea. In 1340 owing to difficulties which he got into with neutral powers, who complained of the depredations of English privateers, the court of admiralty was created with prize jurisdiction in such cases. The first mention of prize courts is in 1357. Attempts were made by the common law courts to retain their jurisdiction but it soon became recognized that sea matters were properly under the control of the admiralty. In 1360 one admiral was appointed for all the fleets in the person of Sir John Beauchamp. The duties of the office were greatly extended, in fact it claimed so wide a jurisdiction that in the reign of Richard II two statutes were passed greatly limiting the Admiral's power.

The office of admiral was of a two-fold character. He was not only commander-in-chief of the navy and as such entitled to share in prizes, but also he exercised the king's power of jurisdiction over the sea and in this capacity presided over the courts of admiralty and the prize courts. In the latter capacity the connection of the admiral with the privy council was very close. He was himself a member of the privy council and that body always exercised final jurisdiction in prize cases if it saw fit. It should be understood that no normal adjudication of all prizes was at this time required. In the Black Book of the Admiralty the admiral was given vigorous means of collecting his perquisites, "inquiry is to be made of all ships, who have not paid the admiral his share, the names of the captors, masters, owners and value of goods taken is to be presented." Thus it was only in special cases where the admiral had heard of a capture and had not received a share or where some party made a complaint, that a case was adjudicated. The great majority of cases never came before the court and the captor had undisturbed possession.

The apparent insufficiency of the admiralty in prize cases brought forth a new set of officers in 1414, the Conservators of the Ports. These officers had criminal and prize jurisdiction in maritime cases but the plan seems to have been attended with small success and soon fell into desuetude.

Through this period the Cinque Ports maintained to some extent their ancient privileges. The Warden of the Ports exercised the function of admiral over mariners sailing from them. Nominally he was under the authority of the Lord High Admiral but as a matter of fact he exercised an almost independent jurisdiction until 1628.

As noted the issue of letters of Marque by the privy council was authorized by statute but the carriage of such letters by privateers does not seem to have been universally required, especially in war. Efforts were made to restrain privateering by law for the benefit of neutrals.

c. Significance.

What accounts for England's very early adoption in theory at least of these advanced principles of maritime law? England's insular position turned her people to the sea and commerce. The French wars necessitated a continuous military and naval policy. It also brought about internal unity and nationalism much earlier than in other countries. Thus the state definitely organized and regulated the navy. The great naval victories and the assumption by the king of the title "master of the seas" increased the spirit of nationalism and naval pride. There was however, a conflict between "the rights of the king as sovereign lord of the sea entitled to demand for offence and defence the service of all his subjects; the privileged corporations of the sea port towns with their peculiar customs and great local independence; and the private adventure of independent merchants and mariners whose proceedings seem to be scarcely one degree removed from piracy." But as we have noted the king emerged from the conflict victorious. The office of Lord High Admiral of all the seas was created, the navy came to be considered a definite branch of the royal administration. A royal navy was built up under Henry IV and Henry V. The king affirmed his right to prize and his right of jurisdiction over privateers and their captures.

But along with England's aggressive naval policy was her dependence upon commerce. Successful commerce necessitated strict recognition of neutral rights and a rule of order at sea, embracing the destruction of piracy and illegal privateering. Thus the king established the admiralty as a prize court, made treaties binding himself to the protection of neutral rights, demanded adjudication of all prizes, and sought by ordinance to restrain illegal privateering. After the reign of Henry V the commercial interests of England won the upper hand, the royal navy was sold, the naval protection was placed in the hands of commissioned merchant privateers and more strict enforcement of neutral rights was sought. Thus the conflict between an aggressive naval policy and the protection and encouragement of commerce brought about a very early recognition in England of advanced principles of prize capture and distribution.

Through the latter half of the fifteenth century, England was too distraught by internal struggles to pay much attention to naval matters and no progress was made in prize money laws.

It is impossible to tell specifically the effects of the prize money laws in England at this early date. However, in so far as they formed an important element in the general maritime laws, they undoubtedly tended to create order at sea, to protect commerce and to increase the king's jurisdiction over the sea forces. This coordination of authority over sea war would tend to increase naval efficiency and was an important element in making England a great sea power.

NOTES.

Chapter III, Part 2.

Black Book of the Admiralty, Rolls Series, No. 55, i, 21.

Ibid. i, 31.

Cal. Pat. Ric. II, 1385-1389, pp. 216, 253.

Cal. Pat. Ric. II, 1385-1389, pp. 339, 342.

Rotuli Parliamentorum, 7 Vols., London, 1767-1777, iii, 570, art. 22.

Royal Commission of Historical Manuscripts, Reports, v, 501.

4 Hen. V, c 7, 1416.

In a case of Reprisals against France, Cromwell returned the excess over damages to the French ambassador, see Carnazza-Amari, Traité de Droit International Public en Temps de Paix, French translation from Italian by Montanari-Revest, 2 Vols., Paris, 1880, ii, 599. Also in Phillimore, Commentaries on International Law, 3rd Edition, 4 Vols., London, 1885, iii, 33.

Rymer, op. cit. x, 368.

Rot. Par. v, 59, art. 30; see also Acts of the Privy Council, Sir Harris Nicolas, Editor, v, 128.

20 Hen VI, c 1, 1442.

"The Laws of Oleron are the ancient usages, generally received from Richard I, on his return from the Holy Land to Oleron, revised and approved for matters marine and which all the people of the west afterwards received for their affairs." Sir Leoline Jenkins, Life of, by Wynne, i, 87, quoted in Comyn's Digest, i, 272; Marsdon doubts whether

Richard had anything to do with the origin of the Laws of Oleron, Introduction to select pleas of the admiralty, Seldon Series, vi; See also discussion by Twiss, Sea Laws, Encyclopedia Britannica, 11th Edition, xxiii, 535.

See ante p 34.

Black Book of the Admiralty, Rolls Series, No. 55, i, 145.

Ibid. i, 135.

Nicolas, Introduction to Acts of the Privy Council, v, 136.

See ante p 26.

Bynkershoek, Questiones Juris Publica, quoted in Phillimore, op. cit. iii, 209.

Rymer, op. cit. vi, 15.

13 Ric. II, c 5, 1390; 15 Ric. II, c 3, 1392.

Black Book of the Admiralty, i, 151.

2 Hen V, St. 1, c 6, 1414.

William Stubbs, The Constitutional History of England, 5th Edition, 3 Vols., Oxford, 1903, ii, 289.

PART 3. 1485-1603.

a. Laws.

After the wars of the roses prize distribution was still occasionally decreed by special letters patent. In his famous voyage of 1496 John Cabot was by letter patent required to give one fifth of all prizes to the king. In 1512 the admiral guaranteed to turn over to the king one half of "all manner of gaynes and wynnyngs of werre". This rule was repeated in 1521. Frequently the charters of vessels authorized them to take prizes. The charter party of the ship "Cheritie" dated 1531 says: "and yff the sayd shyppe take any pryse, purchase any flotson or lagen, hit shalbe devyded into III equal parties, that ys to the sayd capmerchaunte the one parte and to the owner the second parte and to the master and his companye the therde parte." Similarly the charter party of the "George", 1535, provided that: "If any prize, purches, flotezon, or lagason or any other casueltie happe to be taken by the saide ships in this her present viage the saide merchaunt shall have his juste parte thereof accordyng to the lawe of

Oleron." In the rule of 1544 mariners carrying letters of marque were granted the whole of their prizes without accounting to the admiral or warden of the ports for any. A similar proclamation was issued by Mary in her French wars of 1557. With few exceptions however the admiral had a right to one tenth of all prizes.

Elizabeth increased this share to one third in the case of captures made by the queen's ships but it remained one tenth in the case of privateers. In 1585 Elizabeth issued a proclamation authorizing the Lord High Admiral to issue letters of reprisal to all who showed that they had suffered losses from Spain. Rules for distribution of proceeds and for the conduct of privateers were included. Similar proclamations have been issued by the sovereign of England at the beginning of every subsequent war in which privateering was allowed. The proclamation provided for the division of the proceeds, one third to the owners, one third to the victualer, and one third to the officers and crew. The captain also was entitled to the best piece of ordnance and the master the best anchor and cable. Officers and crew were especially granted the right of pillage on the decks. In 1589 Elizabeth was in alliance with Henry IV of France. A remarkable proclamation of this time authorized English subjects to take letters of marque from the French king and provided that he should be entitled to one fifth of the proceeds of all prizes.

b. Administration.

Thus during the Tudor period new developments of prize money law were found. During the period and especially the latter part of it, England's policy was one of extreme naval aggressiveness. But instead of being restrained by the commercial necessities of the previous epoch it was increased by the renaissance spirit of adventure. England's national unity was established, the enthusiasm of discovery, the experience of immemorial acquaintance with the sea impelled her people into an unparalleled career of sea conquest. Thus during the Elizabethan period it is not surprising to find a retrogression in prize law. Belligerent rights were enforced at the expense of neutrals. Naval warfare was almost exclusively in the hands of privateers. The admiral still retained his right to a tenth of prizes, the queen received a varying share, but the greater part went to the privateers and at no time was there a definite rule of distribution. While she publicly disavowed illegal depredations by her privateers Elizabeth secretly encouraged them.

The actual control of the crown over prize matters does not seem to have been lost. Illegal depredation of privateers was not due to inability of the administration to control them but to the definite policy of the crown. The high court of admiralty was revived in 1524 after a period of dormancy during the civil wars and its definite records date from that time. It exercised a constant prize jurisdiction. In 1558 the case of Gonner vs. Pattyson came before it. Gonner obtained a decree granting him a vessel on the plea that "he by right of war captured as lawful prize the said ship— belonging to Scotchmen, foes and enemies of this famous realm of England—and that the captors were and are by reason of the premises true owners and proprietors thereof." In Matthews vs. Goyte, 1565, the sentence decreed division between joint captors. In 1577 a definite effort was made to suppress piracy. A commission was appointed to judge and summarily punish pirates with rather effective results.

Regular adjudication of prize cases was not yet the rule. Cases were only tried on complaint of one of the parties but in 1589 an order in council directed that all prizes be brought in for adjudication by the admiralty. The privy council itself however exercised jurisdiction in many cases. Thus in 1589 John Gilbert and Walter Raleigh were given a commission to capture prizes on a certain voyage and divide them among the crew. Apparently they appropriated the prizes themselves. A complaint was made to the queen. The matter was considered in the privy council with the result that Raleigh and Gilbert were commanded to appear and tell how the money had been disposed of and especially to answer for the part due the queen. And again: On the return of the fleet with prizes after the destruction of the Spanish armada, in 1589, the privy council gave orders directing the handling of the prizes. Instructions were given to Sir Anthony Ashley to investigate the prizes and determine the country of the ship, the amount and value of the cargo, etc. In the same year on hearing that certain prizes had been sold and distributed by the captain the queen was very angry and "tooke yt in very ill parte that anie persons would adventure to receive or buy anie of those goodes before aucthorytie or direction was given for the sake of the same."

In the latter part of Elizabeth's reign vigorous efforts were made to restrain privateers. In 1601 a new commission was appointed to hear and arbitrate neutral claims. In 1602 by proclamation judges of the admiralty were directed to institute proceedings against any privateer sailing without commission or selling prizes before adjudication. In this year the ship "Fortune" was confiscated to the admiralty for failing to bring in a prize for adjudication. This stand is most advanced and shows that progress was being made toward a definite requirement of legal process before prizes could be distributed. A case of similar nature had occurred in 1598. The vessel "Grace of Padstow" without a letter of reprisal captured a Danish prize. The prize was returned by the court on the grounds that the captor had no commission. This extreme enforcement of the obligation of privateers to carry specific commissions has been advocated by some international law writers. However in cases of actual war, prizes have never been returned but as in this instance in cases of private reprisal the return of captures was occasionally enforced.

Thus while in the greater part of the Tudor period the laws of prize distribution were not so clearly defined as formerly and great freedom was allowed adventurers and privateers, at the same time the actual control of distribution by the administration seems to have been more strict than ever before. Especially was this true of the latter part of the reign of Elizabeth.

c. Significance.

The effect of the generous laws of distribution of this period undoubtedly was to encourage adventure and privateering. The voyages of the great sea captains of Elizabeth were fitted out primarily for the sake of private gain from prizes. Preying on Spanish Galleons not only satisfied the love of adventure of such men as Hawkins, Drake and Raleigh but it also gave them wealth. So long as their acts harmonized with the queen's policy she did not care to inquire too closely into the strict legality of all their seizures. This policy by which the queen not only made the navy support itself but actually received income from it through her share of prizes enabled Elizabeth to carry on her wars without any national expense. Her reign is renowned for its economy and lack of taxation. This doubtless added to its popularity and increased the sense of nationalism in the English nation. During this period generous giving of prize money was a valuable means of increasing the efficiency of the navy and the national unity of England. The strict acts of the latter part of Elizabeth's reign and their consistent enforcement indicated genuine progress in the protection of neutral rights at sea through governmental control.

NOTES.

Chapter III, Part 3.

Political History of England, William Hunt and Reginald Poole, Editors, 12 Vols., London, 1910, v, 106.

Rymer, Op. cit. xiii, 1326.

Henry VIII, Letters and Papers, Foreign and Domestic, Master of the Rolls, Great Britain, Director, 1524-1526, p. 33.

Select Pleas of the Admiralty, Seldon Series, vi, 37.

Ibid, vi, 82.

Marsdon, English Historical Review, xxiv, 684.

Calendar of State Papers, Domestic, Mary, 1547-1580, p. 93.

G. W. Prothero, Select Statutes and Other Documents, 3rd Edition, Oxford, 1906, p. 464.

Marsdon, English Historical Review, xxiv, 689, 697, also Prothero, op. cit. p. 465.

Marsdon, English Historical Review, xxiv, 689, 697.

Select Pleas of the Admiralty, Seldon Series, xi, 107.

Ibid. xi, 130.

Ibid. xi, 17.

Acts of the Privy Council, 1588-1589, New Series, xvii, 283, 413.

Ibid. xvii, 357.

Marsdon, English Historical Review, xxiv, 696.

Select Pleas of the Admiralty, Seldon Series, xi, 204.

Marsdon, English Historical Review, xxiv, 696.

Vattel, The Law of Nations, English translation from French by Joseph Chitty, Philadelphia, 1883, p. 285.

PART 4, 1603-1688.

a. Laws.

Instructions to privateers similar to Elizabeth's proclamation of 1585 were issued in 1625. In instructions of 1628 the king's tenth of prizes is referred to. During the civil war the two contending parties each issued proclamations authorizing letters of marque. In 1643 an ordinance of parliament provided that captures made by privateers after adjudication in the admiralty court and payment of tenths and customs should belong to the captors. Similar acts were passed in 1644 and 1645. More extensive provisions were made in an act of 1648. Prize bounty of ten pounds per gun for every enemy vessel destroyed was for the first time granted in an act of this same year. An elaborate parliamentary enactment of 1649 provided for division of prize between the captors, the state, the sick, wounded and the relatives of the slain. A man of war captured by a state ship was divided, one half to the officers and crew, and one half to the sick and wounded. If the enemy vessel was destroyed a gun money or bounty of ten to twenty pounds for each gun on the destroyed ship was distributed in the same manner. If the vessel captured was a merchant ship, one third went to the captors, one third to the state and one third to the sick and wounded. In the case of a privateer making the capture, one third went to the officers and crew, one third to the sick and wounded, one sixth to the owner and one sixth to the state. Recaptures were to be returned to the original owner on the payment of one eighth salvage. The customary Admiral's one-tenth was to be paid into the state treasury and used for the purchase of medals.

Piracy was extremely prevalent at that time. Adherents of Prince Rupert plundered British vessels without scruple. A successful effort to stop such depredations was made in 1650. The authorizing act provided for division of the captured pirate vessels at the rate of one half to the state, one third to the owner and one sixth to the officers and crew. In a declaration of 1652 the admiralty forbade the old custom of pillage on deck, demanding that the prize be brought in to port intact, but the order seems to have proved impossible of execution and after the Restoration the old custom was revived.

An ordinance of 1660 authorized the capture as prize of vessels breaking the provisions of the navigation act and provided for the division of such prizes, one half to the captors and one half to the state. The navigation act of 1663 provided for the adjudication of such prizes in the vice admiralty courts of the colonies. The division of the proceeds was to be one-third to the colonial governor, one-third to the king and one-third to the captors.

Shortly after the restoration of Charles II in 1661 an act was passed by parliament for the regulation of the navy. Among other things it forbids spoil of prizes before adjudication but especially permits pillage on the decks. In 1749 this act was amended and the ancient practice of giving up the decks to plunder was finally forbidden.

In ordinances issued before the Dutch war of 1664 and the French war of 1666 all prizes were granted to the captors with the sole reservation of the admiral's tenth. Prizes were also liable to payment of customs duties. An order in council of the latter date defined the rights of the king and admiral in prizes "bona inimicorum". To the king by Jure Coronae belonged all prizes driven into harbor by the king's ships, seized in port before war broke out coming into port voluntarily or deserting from the enemy. To the Lord High Admiral by Droits of admiralty belonged ships captured at sea by non-commissioned captors, salvage due for ships recaptured from the enemy, and ships forsaken by the crew unless in the presence of the king's ships. In other cases the rule of the ordinance held good, the admiral received only his tenth and the king his customs duties the remainder going to the captors.

b. Administration.

From this brief resumé of the legislation of the seventeenth century it is evident that the laws, reached, during this period, a certain definiteness and stability which they had before lacked. In 1628 the office of Lord High Admiral was temporarily put in commission and given a more systematic organization. From this time the prize cases of the court are recorded on separate records and condemnation before distribution of prizes was the rule. Sir Leoline Jenkins says "And the Admiral may inquire if any defraud the king of his prizes, or the admiral of his one tenth part or buy or receive prize goods or break bulk before they are condemned as prize or there be a decree for an appraisement or sale."

The prestige of the admiralty was increased through the fact that the Warden of the Cinque Ports, Zouche, sold out his right to Lord High Admiral Buckingham in 1624. From this time the Courts of admiralty were virtually supreme in maritime jurisdiction. Thus Jenkins said, "The Admiralty has jurisdiction over offences, super altum mare, punishable by laws of Oleron, laws of admiralty, or laws or statutes of the realm." The Cinque ports still retained jurisdiction over certain matters. During the latter part of the seventeenth century through the adverse pressure of the crown on the side of its prize jurisdiction and of the common law courts on the side of its instance jurisdiction the authority and prestige of the admiralty court greatly declined.

The civil wars of the middle Stuart period precluded a possibility of prize-law development, rather it encouraged piracy and maintained disorder. Parliamentarians and royalists authorized unrestrained privateering against the opposition. During the Stuart exile, Prince Rupert was at the head of an organized system of piracy. The Puritan regime and the restoration period however witnessed a marked advance in the legalizing of maritime methods. The Puritans stood for law and popular control. They did much to crush piracy, required the [53a]carriage of letters of marque by privateers and the first act of parliament touching prize distribution appeared at this time. It is to be noted however that while the government claimed prior rights in prizes and demanded legal adjudication; in behalf of a forward naval policy it displayed exceptional generosity to the captors, in its rule of division of proceeds. Not only did all the prize go to the captors but in addition bounty was granted in case of the destruction or capture of armed vessels and medals were awarded for specially meritorious acts. The extreme effort of the Puritans to enforce legality at sea is evidenced by the effort to abolish the old custom of pillage on deck and the great number of prize cases settled in the court of admiralty at this period. During this time Zouche of Oxford published his great work on international law and did much to crystallize legal views on prize matters.

The restoration period carried out the same principles in general except that with the restoration of the office of Lord High Admiral the old Droits d'Admiralty were revived. In these periods the humane policy of apportioning a share of the prizes to the sick, wounded and heirs of the slain was instituted, a policy continued in the later practice of maintaining a naval hospital at Greenwich with the proceeds of forfeited shares of prize money. In 1690 the whole privy council was constituted a court of appeal in prize cases. Vice Admiralty courts with prize jurisdiction had been established in the colonies. The colonial governor was usually the Vice Admiral of the colony. The great trading companies were usually granted large rights of reprisal but adjudication was required in the court of admiralty. In 1690 the king received the admiral's share of one tenth in a case involving a prize of 100,000 pounds captured by the East India Company from the great Mogul.

The legislation of the seventeenth century gave complete recognition to the Grotian principles of prize distribution and in practice these laws seem to have been applied regularly and consistently by well established legal institutions.

NOTES.

Chapter III, Part 4.

Cal. St. Pap. Dom. Jac. I, 1623-1625, p. 476.

Cal. St. Pap. Dom. Car. I, 1625-1626, p. 142.

Marsden, English Historical Review, xxv, 253.

Henry Scobell, A Collection of Acts and Ordinances, London, 1658, 1649, c 21, p. 9.

Ibid. c 21, p. 9.

Ibid. 1648, c 12, p. 4.

Ibid. 1648, c 15, p. 7.

Ibid. 1649, c 21, p. 9.

Marsden, English Historical Review, xxvi, 40.

Ibid. xxvi, 41.

Acts of the Privy Council, Colonial, i, 302.

15 Car. II, c 7, s 6, 1663; Provision was first made for establishing Vice Admiralty courts in the patent to James, Duke of York, Lord High

Admiral, in 1662. Governor Windsor established a court at Jamaica in this year, Cal. St. Pap. Col. America and West Indies, 1661-1668, p. 112, s 379; Marsdon, English Historical Review, xxvi, 53.

13 Car. II, c 9, s 7, 1661.

Marsdon, English Historical Review, xxvi, 44.

Ibid. xxvi, 45.

Ibid. xxvi, 47, see also Phillimore, op. cit. iii, 600.

Sir Leoline Jenkins, Life of, by Wynne, i, 88, quoted in Comyn's Digest, i, 271.

Cal. St. Pap. Dom. Jac. I, 1623-1625, p. 304.

Sir Leoline Jenkins, Life of, by Wynne, i, 87, quoted in Comyn's Digest, i, 272.

See Ante p. 24.

54 Geo. III, c 93, s 72, 1814.

Marsdon, English Historical Review, xxvi, 53; Cal. St. Pap. Dom. 1690-1691, p. 92.

Ibid. xxvi, 53.

Ibid. xxvi, 55.

CHAPTER IV. GREAT BRITAIN, RECENT LAWS.

After the revolution of 1688 English methods of legislation became in many cases crystallized into their present form. This was true of prize money law. In 1692 the first statute granting prize money to the captors was passed, for the purpose as the bill stated of encouraging privateers in the pending war with France.

In connection with instructions for privateers issued in 1693 provision was made that prize ships taken by privateers should go to the captors but the king was entitled to one-fifth of the goods on board, the other four-fifths going to the captors. Prizes taken by king's or hired ships went, one-third to the widows and children of the slain, the sick and the wounded; one-third to the officers and crew; and one-third to the king. Gun money of five pounds a gun was granted for capturing or destroying a man of war in addition to the prize money. Recaptured ships were to be returned after payment of salvage of one-third to one-eighth according to the time the vessel had been in the enemy's possession.

With the outbreak of the war of the Spanish succession the statutory method of providing for prize distribution was established. By a statute of 1707 the sole property in all prizes was granted to the officers and seamen of queen's ships and the officers, seamen and owners of privateers, the capture being first adjudged good prize in a court of admiralty. The act also provided for the payment of head money or bounty to the amount of five pounds per man on board every war ship or privateer of the enemy, sunk or destroyed. The act was to continue only for that war. Orders in council issued on authority of the act provided details for the conduct of prize courts and the division of prize money and bounty among the captors. In reference to this act and the previous history of prize money in England, Lord Loughborough said in 1789, "Before the sixth year of the reign of Queen Anne there were no laws made on the subject. Previous to that time all prizes taken in war were of right vested in the crown and questions concerning the property of such prizes were not the subject of discussion in courts of law. But in order to do justice to claimants from the first year after the restoration of Charles II, special commissions were issued to enable courts of Admiralty to condemn such captures as appeared to be lawful prizes, to give relief where there was no color for the taking and generally to make satisfaction to parties injured. But in the sixth year of

Queen Anne it was thought proper for the encouragement of seamen to vest in them the prizes they should take and for that purpose the statutes of 6 Anne c 13 and c 37 were passed." From the foregoing discussion it appears that the learned judge failed to note the statute 4-5 Wm. and Mary c 25 passed in 1692 not to mention the commonwealth statutes of 1648 and 1649. It also seems clear that admiralty courts exercised jurisdiction over prize matters long before the restoration of Charles II.

Queen Anne's act of 1707 is typical of those which have been passed at the beginning of every subsequent war in English history until the passage of the permanent prize act of 1864. Since that time the principle of giving the total proceeds of prize to the captors has been adhered to although the principle that the initial title to all captures vests in the crown has been maintained with equal consistency.

Another act of 1707 extended the act previously mentioned to captures made in America and provided for prize jurisdiction in colonial courts of vice admiralty. The outbreak of the war of the Austrian succession brought forth the prize act of 1740. This added to Queen Anne's act the provision that vessels recaptured should be restored to the original owners on the payment of one eighth salvage. A new act was passed in 1744 which repeated the former acts adding provisions in regard to privateers. It was provided that captures by privateers should belong to the ship exclusively and division between the owners and crew should be regulated by special contract between them. The admiralty was authorized to issue letters of Marque on receiving of satisfactory bond of good behaviour from the owners.

The act of 1756 repeated the provisions of the preceding act with reference to the Seven Years war, as did the act of 1776 with reference to the American Revolution and the acts of 1779, 1780, and 1781 passed on the outbreak of hostilities with France, Spain and Holland, respectively. In the act passed in 1793 to regulate prize matters in the French war a few new provisions were added. Captures on land were put under the jurisdiction of the admiralty and similar principles of division authorized. Joint captures by land and naval forces were to be divided by special orders in council. Recaptures were to be returned on paying a salvage of one-eighth in case the capture was made by a public vessel, and one-sixth if made by a privateer. The duration of this act was extended by an act of 1797. At the outbreak of war with America a prize proclamation was issued, Oct. 26, 1812. It provided "That the net produce of all prizes taken, the right whereof is inherent in His Majesty and his crown be given to the takers". Rules were then given for the division among the officers and crew. An act of 1813 authorized this proclamation and an act of the following year gave complete rules for prize distribution. Aside from the matters covered in previous acts it provided that all prize money shares not claimed or forfeited should go to the support of the Greenwich naval hospital. An elaborate scheme for the division of shares was included. By this scheme the proceeds of prizes taken before 1808 were to be divided into five shares, besides the flag shares, which were to be divided among five grades of seamen. Those taken after 1808 were to be divided into eight shares and in the same manner distributed among eight grades of seamen. The sizes of vessels were evidently increasing rapidly, to necessitate this change in the number of grades of mariners.

In 1815 a very elaborate act was called forth by the return of Napoleon from Elba, entitled "an act for the encouragement of seamen and the more effectual manning of his majesty's navy during the present war." It provided that the flag officers, commanders and crew should have sole right in all prizes taken by public armed vessels declared lawful prize before courts of admiralty or vice admiralty to be divided in proportions from time to time decreed by orders in council. Hired armed vessels were subject to the same rules. Captures made with aid of allies were to be divided equally with the ally. Land captures made by the navy were also the sole property of the captors after proper adjudication, but joint captures by land and naval forces were to be subject to special order in council. Desertion, forfeited shared of prize money. Recaptures were to be returned to the original owner on the payment of one-eighth salvage if the captor was a public vessel and one-sixth if a private vessel, except that if the recaptured vessel had been fitted out by the enemy as a war ship it should not be returned to the original owner but should be declared good prize for the benefit of the captors. Head money or bounty of five pounds per man on board every enemy ship at the beginning of an engagement was to be paid all vessels capturing, sinking or destroying a war ship or privateer of the enemy. Ransom of captured vessels was forbidden except in case of necessity. All money given as bounty or salvage was to be subject to the same rules of division as prize money. Letters of Marque were to be granted on proper security for good behavior and the privateers were to be sole proprietors of all captures after proper adjudication. The force of this act only extended to the pending war.

During the middle of the nineteenth century England was engaged in an active campaign to suppress the slave trade. As a result proclamations were constantly issued decreeing the division of the proceeds of vessels captured in this trade. The same rules were followed as in the case of prizes of war, the whole of the captures being given to the captor after adjudication. Such proclamations were issued in 1834, 1846, 1849 and were authorized by a statute passed in 1839 and amended in 1842.

In the Crimean war of 1854 England followed her old policy in prize distribution. The act of 1815 was practically reenacted. In addition it was provided that for any breach of her majesty's instructions or the law of nations the shares of prize money would be forfeited to the crown. In this war Great Britain was in alliance with France and an interesting treaty was entered into by the two countries providing for the division of prizes between them. Prizes were to be adjudicated by the courts of the country of the officer in superior command in the engagement. Joint captors in sight were to share but adjudication was always to be by the country of the ship making the actual capture. If vessels of one of the allies were captured for illicit trade it was to be tried by the country of the captured vessel. In case of vessels of the two countries acting in conjunction or of vessels of the two countries giving constructive assistance the net proceeds were to be divided to the several vessels according to the number of men on board irrespective of rank. Distribution was to be regulated by the municipal laws of each country. The treaty also contained instruction for bringing in prizes. A similar treaty was entered into by France and Great Britain in their joint expedition against China in 1860.

NOTES.

Chapter IV, Part 1.

4 and 5 William and Mary, c 25, 1692.

Marsdon, English Historical Review, xxvi, 51.

6 Anne, c 13, 1707.

Brymer vs Atkins, 1 H. Blacks, 189; 126 Eng. Rep. 97; see also Phillimer, op. cit. iii, 576.

13 Car. II, c 9, 1661.

27 and 28 Vict. c 25, 1864.

6 Anne, c 37, 1707.

13 Geo. II, c 4, 1740.

17 Geo. II, c 34, 1744.

29 Geo. II, c 34, 1756; 32 Geo. II, c 25, 1759.

16 Geo. III, c 5, 1776.

19 Geo. III, c 67, 1779.

20 Geo. III, c 23, 1780.

21 Geo. III, c 15, 1781.

33 Geo. III, c 66, 1793.

37 Geo. III, c 109, 1797.

State Papers, Foreign and Domestic, i, 1348.

53 Geo. III, c 63, 1813.

54 Geo. III, c 93, 1814.

55 Geo. III, c 160, 1815.

State Papers, xx, 1214.

Ibid. xxxiv, 438.

Ibid. xxxix, 1252.

2 and 3 Vict., c 73, 1839.

5 and 6 Vict., c 91, 1842.

17 Vict., c 18, 1854.

De Martens, Nouveau Recueil General de Traités, xv, 580.

Ibid. xx, 460.

PART 2. 1864-1913.

Prize distribution in Great Britain at present is authorized by two permanent acts passed in 1864. The first of these acts known as the "Naval agency and distribution act of 1864" provides that all salvage, bounty and prize money be distributed according to proclamation or order in council and that the shares in which such distribution shall occur be determined in the same manner. Pursuant to this act a proclamation was issued August 3, 1886 providing that the whole of prizes legally adjudicated be for the benefit of officers and seamen making the capture and that the flag officers receive one-thirtieth of the proceeds and the captain one-tenth. The remainder is to be divided equally among eleven grades of officers and seamen. This rule has been superseded by an Order in Council of September 17, 1900 shortly after the outbreak of the South African war. It provides that only ships within sight so as to cause intimidation of the enemy are to share in prize money as joint captors. All bounty, salvage and prize money received for any action are to be in general divided in the same manner. The flag officer is to receive one-thirtieth of the prize but no share of bounty, unless actually present at the capture. The captain in actual command receives one-tenth. The remainder is divided among eleven grades of officers and men as before.

The other act now in force regulating prize matter is the "Naval Prize Act of 1864". It provides for prize courts and prescribes their procedure, these matters however have been amended by "the prize courts act of 1894". In joint captures by land and naval forces prize courts have jurisdiction. In cases of the infraction of municipal or international law all proceeds of the prize go to the government, notwithstanding any grant that may have been made to the captors. Ships taken as prize by any ship other than a regular ship of war enure solely to the government. This provision effectually abolishes privateering. Recaptured ships are to be returned to the original owner if an English subject on payment of from one-eighth to one-fourth salvage unless they have been fitted out by the enemy as ships of war when they will be considered good prize. If prize bounty is granted in any war by proclamation the officers and crew actually present at the taking or destroying of any armed ship of the enemy are entitled to bounty calculated at the rate of five pounds for each person on board the enemy's ship at the beginning of the engagement. The saving clause of the act states that "nothing in this act shall give to the officers and crew of any of her majesty's ships of war any right or claim in or to any ship or goods taken as prize or the proceeds thereof, it being the intent of this act that such officers and crews shall consent to take only such interest (if any) in the proceeds of prizes as may be from time to time granted to them by the crown." The principle that original title to all prize vests in the crown is thus distinctly asserted.

Perhaps the best exposition of the present rules for the conduct of prizes and the distribution of the proceeds from them is contained in the instructions to naval officers which have been authoritatively issued in England, based on the statutes and orders mentioned. Such a code was prepared by Mr. Godfrey Lushington in 1866 and revised by Prof. T. E. Holland in 1888. It contains the following provisions bearing on bounty, prize salvage and prize money.

"247—When any ship or vessel shall be captured or detained her hatches are to be securely fastened and sealed and her lading and furniture and in general everything on board are to be carefully secured from embezzlement. The officers placed in charge of her shall prevent anything from being taken out of her until she has been tried and sentence shall have been passed on her in a court of prize.

"250—If any ship or vessel shall be taken acting as a ship of war or privateer without having a commission duly authorizing her to do so, a full report of all particulars is at once to be made to the admiralty.

"252—The ship to which a prize strikes her flag is the actual captor. Other ships may be held by the prize court to share as joint captors on the ground either of association or cooperation with the actual captor.

"253—If ships are associated or cooperating together a capture made by one enures to the benefit of all.

"255—Ships being in sight of the prize as also of the captor under circumstances to cause intimidation to the prize and encouragement to the captor are held to be cooperating with the actual captor.

"259—In the case of captures made jointly by British and allied ships of war the duties of the respective commanders are usually regulated by treaty.

"263—Upon adjudication the prize court will order the vessel and cargo to be restored to their respective owners upon payment by them of prize salvage.

"266—The prize salvage which will be awarded to the recaptors for the recapture of any British vessel before she has been carried into an enemy's port is one-eighth part of the value of the prize or in case the recapture has been made under circumstances of special difficulty or danger a sum not exceeding one-fourth part of the value.

"267—If however the vessel has before her recapture been set forth or used by the enemy as a ship of war, then upon recapture the original owner is not entitled to restitution, but both vessel and cargo will be condemned as lawful prize to the recaptor.

"269—It may happen that an enemy vessel which has been captured by a British cruiser is afterwards lost to an enemy's cruiser and finally recaptured by another British cruiser. The commander effecting such a recapture should send in the vessel for adjudication and the original captors are not entitled to restitution, but both vessel and cargo would be condemned as lawful prize to the recaptors.

"270—If a commander recapture from the enemy a neutral vessel which would not have been liable to condemnation in the prize court of the enemy he is not entitled to salvage and should without delay and without taking ransom, set her free to prosecute her voyage.

"271—If a commander recapture from the enemy an allied vessel his duty is generally regulated by treaty. In default of treaty regulations he will send her into a British port for adjudication and the prize court will award salvage or not according as the prize court of the ally would or would not have awarded salvage to an allied ship for recapturing a British vessel."

NOTES.

Chapter IV, Part 2.

27 and 28 Vict., c 24, Chitty's Statutes, Lely, Editor, London, 1895, tit. Navy, viii, 1, Phillimore, op. cit. iii, 902.

State Papers, lxxvii, 1189.

Statutory Rules and Orders, Revised, London, 1904, tit. Navy, ix, 109.

27 and 28 Vict., c 25, printed in L. Oppenheim, International Law, London, 1906, ii, 541; Wheaton, International Law, Boyd, Editor, 3rd English Edition, London, 1889, p. 750; Phillimore, op. cit. iii, 908.

57 and 58 Vict., c 59, 1894; Chitty's Statutes, tit. Admiralty, i, 43.

Manual of Naval Prize Law, London, 1866.

Manual of Naval Prize Law, London, 1888.

Quoted in Atherley-Jones, Commerce in War, London, 1907, pp. 575-645.

CHAPTER V. GREAT BRITAIN, RECENT ADMINISTRATION.

In regard to the actual administration of these laws of prize distribution the decisions of prize courts in cases where the questions of distribution have arisen furnish the most satisfactory clue to the practice.

It may be well to devote a short space to a consideration of the organization of courts exercising prize jurisdiction. As previously noted, in early times the admiralty jurisdiction, both administrative and judicial was placed in the charge of one man, the Lord High Admiral of England. There were it is true certain favored localities which claimed exemption from his jurisdiction. Such were the Cinque Ports which exercised coordinate jurisdiction through their Warden of the Cinque Ports. To this day the Cinque Ports retain this privilege in some matters, especially questions of civil salvage but in prize matters, the Warden early lost his authority.

As time went on the Office of Lord High Admiral began to lose its character of a personal prerogative especially in the judicial field. The admiralty courts came under the authority of the king. They exercised instance and prize jurisdiction without distinction but in the middle of the seventeenth century the court began to have separate sittings for the two jurisdictions possibly because of the conflict between the Droits of the Duke of York as Lord High Admiral and of King Charles II.

The administrative duties of the office of Lord High Admiral were also absorbed by the crown. Throughout the seventeenth century the office of Admiral was frequently put in commission. That is, the Lord High Admiral's jurisdiction was retaken by the king and commissioners were appointed by him to exercise the duties of the office. By act of 1690 express provision was made for thus disposing of the office of admiralty and for the most part it has been in commission since. From this time, therefore, the organization of the department of admiralty and of admiralty courts has been directly under the control of the crown in parliament and acts providing for the institution of prize courts and the distribution of prize money have been passed by them generally before each war as previously indicated.

The history of the admiralty courts of England has been the history of a struggle between them and the common law courts, each seeking to increase its jurisdiction at the expense of the other. Acts were passed in the reign of Richard II limiting the power of the admiralty courts. Through the seventeenth and eighteenth centuries their power underwent a constant decline, a fact greatly deplored by Sir Leoline Jenkins one of the judges of the seventeenth century. The common law courts even attempted to usurp their jurisdiction in prize matters. In 1781 however the exclusive jurisdiction of the admiralty in prize matters was recognized. It was at this time that Lord Mansfield as Lord Chief Justice of England was beginning to correlate prize law by his famous decisions in appealed cases. But it was to Sir William Scott, afterwards Lord Stowell, Judge of the admiralty and prize court of England during the Napoleonic wars that the fame of the English Prize Court is largely due. The English Prize Court was at this time regarded almost as an international authority, as is witnessed by the fact that the United States through Ambassador Jay in 1794 requested of England an exposition of prize court procedure for the use of the United States. The reply of Sir William Scott and Sir J. Nicholl embodies nearly all the rules adopted by the United States. Of Lord Stowell's work it has been said, "But his work as a judge of the Prize Court remains to this day distinct and conspicuous and no changes of international law can ever diminish his fame as the creator of a great body of English prize law the only complete and judicially made code in existence among European nations." Through the nineteenth century the English High Court of admiralty under such judges as Dr. Stephen Lushington, Sir Robert Phillimore, and Sir Travers Twiss occupied a position of increasing importance. Its jurisdiction was greatly increased by a statute of 1840. Among other things it was there given power to adjudicate booty of war in the same manner as prize. Its jurisdiction was further enlarged by acts of 1846, 1854, 1861, and 1867. By the Judicature acts of 1873 and 1875 the High Court of Admiralty was incorporated into the High Court of Justice as part of the Probate, Divorce and Admiralty division of that court. The Supreme court of judicature act of 1891 defined the prize jurisdiction of the High Court.

Beginning with the establishment of a court in Jamaica in 1662 Vice Admiralty courts have been established in most of the colonies with jurisdiction similar to that of the courts of admiralty of England. By act of 1832 governors of colonies were made ex-officio vice admirals and the chief justices of the colonial courts, judges of the courts of vice admiralty. This act was amended in 1863 and in 1867. By the Colonial courts of Admiralty act of 1890 all courts of law in British possessions having unlimited civil jurisdiction were created courts of admiralty with jurisdiction equal to that of the Admiralty division of the High court of Justice.

The custom has been to constitute admiralty and vice admiralty courts into prize courts by special commission on the outbreak of war. It has been questioned whether a special commission granting authority to adjudicate prize matters to the admiralty courts is necessary. Blackstone seems to consider the authority inherent. He says:

"In case of prizes also in time of war, between our own nation and another or between two other nations, which are taken at sea and brought into our ports, the courts of admiralty have an undisturbed and exclusive jurisdiction to determine the same according to the laws of nations." Phillimore expresses a similar view. However the general [73a]opinion seems to be that the prize and instance jurisdiction of the admiralty courts are separated and the former is granted only by commission from the crown in time of war. Thus the naval prize act of 1864 provides that all admiralty and vice admiralty courts may be commissioned to act as prize courts during war under the jurisdiction of the high court of admiralty with appeal in all cases to the queen in council.

The Supreme Court of Judicature act of 1891 declared the high court to be a prize court within the meaning of the prize court act of 1864. It therefore is a perpetual prize court and requires no special commission. Other admiralty and vice admiralty courts exercise prize jurisdiction under provisions of the prize courts act of 1894 which declares that commissions for the establishment of prize courts may be issued at any time even during peace by the office of admiralty to become effective on the issuance of a proclamation declaring war. Laws of procedure may likewise be issued at any time by order in council in accordance with the provisions of the naval prize act of 1864.

In earliest times the Lord High Admiral of England and the Warden of the Cinque Ports were the highest appellate authorities in prize cases in their respective jurisdictions. Later, appeal apparently lay to the king in chancery but by 1534 the custom was established of appointing a special commission of appeals. This commission was appointed by the crown and consisted generally of members of the privy council. This condition prevailed until 1833 when the "delegates of appeals" was abolished and it was provided that all admiralty appeals whether instance or prize, should lie to the judicial committee of the privy council. By act of 1832 it had been provided that appeals from all vice admiralty courts lie to the same body. The naval prize act of 1864 likewise provided for appeal to the queen in council.

After the incorporation of the high court of admiralty with the High Court of Justice in 1873 it was provided in the appellate jurisdiction act of 1876 that in its instance jurisdiction appeal lie, as in the other courts, to the High Court of Appeal and then to the House of Lords. Appeal in prize cases however was allowed to remain to the privy council as prescribed by the act of 1864. At present, therefore, appeal from all prize courts of Great Britain lie ultimately to the judicial committee of the privy council.

In the Hague Conference of 1907 a convention providing for an international prize court composed of fifteen judges selected from the leading countries to act as a court of final appeal in prize cases for all nations was adopted. In 1909 the declaration of London signed by the leading maritime nations provided definite rules for many unsettled points of maritime law. Shortly after the meeting of this conference, autumn of 1910, a bill was proposed in the House of Commons to reorganize the English prize procedure so as to allow for appeal to the international court. The bill was defeated. The international prize court has not as yet been organized. At present there is no provision in English law which would permit of appeal to it in case it came into being. Although her delegates signed the Convention at the Hague, England has never officially ratified it and it is difficult to say whether in case of a war Great Britain would feel bound by this convention.

NOTES.

Chapter V, Part 1.

For history and discussion of admiralty and prize courts see Marsdon, Introduction to select pleas of the Admiralty; Roscoe, Growth of English Law; Carter, History of English Legal Institutions; Ridges, Constitutional Laws of England; Benedict, The American Admiralty, Encyclopedia Britannica, 11th Edition, titles, Admiral, Lord High; Admiralty, Jurisdiction.

The local jurisdiction of all sea port corporations but the Cinque Ports was abolished in 1835, 5 and 6 William IV, c 76.

W. G. F. Phillimore, Admiralty, High Court of, Encyclopedia Britannica, 11th Edition, i, 206.

2 William and Mary, St. 2, c 2, 1690.

The Lord High Admirals since 1690 have been, Prince George of Denmark, husband of Queen Anne, 1702-1708; The Earl of Pembroke, 1708-1710; The Duke of Clarence, afterwards, William IV, 1827-1828.

See ante p. 56 et seq.

13 Ric. II, c 5, 1390; 15 Ric. II, c 3, 1392.

Le Caux vs Eden, 2 Doug. 595; 99 Eng. Rep. 375; Lindo vs Rodney, 2 Doug. 613; 99 Eng. Rep. 385. See also Phillimore, op. cit. iii, 213.

See post p. 84.

E. S. Roscoe, The Growth of English Law, London, 1911, p. 139.

3 and 4 Vict., c 65, s 22, 1840.

9 and 10 Vict., c 99, 1846.

17 and 18 Vict., c 104, 1854.

24 and 25 Vict., c 10, 1861.

31 and 32 Vict., c 71, 1868.

36 and 37 Vict., c 66, 1873.

38 and 39 Vict., c 66, 1873.

54 and 55 Vict., c 53, s 4, 1891.

Cal. St. Pap. Col. America and West Indies, 1661-1668, p. 112, s 379; Marsdon, English, Historical Review, xxvi, 53.

2 and 3 William IV, c 51, 1832.

26 and 27 Vict., c 24, 1863.

30 and 31 Vict., c 45, 1867.

53 and 54 Vict., c 27, 1890.

Blackstone, Commentaries, iii, 108.

Phillimore, op. cit. iii, 655; see also post p. 86.

Roscoe, op. cit. p. 125; Hannis Taylor, The Origin and Growth of the English Constitution, 3rd Edition, 2 Vols., Boston, 1895, i, 550.

27 and 28 Vict., c 25, ss 3, 4, 5, 6.

54 and 55 Vict., c 53, s 4, 1891.

27 and 28 Vict., c 25, 1864.

"This Jurisdiction is permanent and unlike that of the prize courts in British possessions requires no commission from his majesty, proclamation of war, or other executive act to bring it into operation." The Earl of Halsbury, The Laws of England, London, 1907-1912, xxiii, 276.

57 and 58 Vict., c 39, 1894.

27 and 28 Vict., c 25, 1864.

25 Hen. VIII, c 19, s 3, 4, 1534.

2 and 3 William IV, c 92, 1833.

2 and 3 William IV, c 52, 1833.

27 and 28 Vict., c 25, 1864.

39 and 40 Vict., c 59, 1876.

27 and 28 Vict., c 25, 1864.

Convention Relative to the Creation of an International Prize Court, Final Acts of the Second International Peace Conference, 1907, No. 12, for text see A. Pearce Higgins, The Hague Peace Conferences; Bentwich, The Declaration of London.

For discussion and text see Norman Bentwich, The Declaration of London; A. Pearce Higgins, The Hague Peace Conferences.

Bentwich, The Declaration of London, p. 35; for text of proposed bill, see ibid. p. 171.

PART 2. THEORY OF DISTRIBUTION.

a. Relation of state and individual.

In considering the present theory of prize money distribution in England and Judicial opinion on the subject, the classification adopted in summarizing the conclusion of the Grotian school of international law writers may be used.

1. The state is the only power that can prosecute war and take prize.

"War must be waged by public authority of the state and carried on through the agency of those who have been duly commissioned for that purpose by that authority" says Phillimore. However this theory appears to be subject to a good deal of modification in practice as for instance in the British treatment of captures made by non-commissioned vessels. England has never given recognition to the theory introduced by Rousseau and prominent in French political theory that war is a conflict between the armed forces of the state only and not between private individuals. This theory maintains that the only participants in war should be the armed representatives of the state, thus non-belligerent nationals of the enemy country and their private property should be exempt from military attack. It seeks to place non-belligerents in practically the same position as neutrals. Carried to its logical conclusion it would lead to the complete abolition of the right of capturing enemy private property at sea, and if not carried to this extreme it is at any rate incompatible with the grant of prize money to individuals for if war is solely a state affair aggrandizement of the individual should not be one of its objects.

This theory of war should be distinguished from the view of Grotius and his contemporaries. The latter holds that war is a state affair and can only be entered into by the state as such but the individual is so closely bound to the state that if the state is enemy so also is the individual that belongs to that state. In other words it recognizes no clear distinction between enemy belligerents and enemy non-belligerents. "Bellum omnum, contra omnes". Grotius however, did recognize state non-belligerency or neutrality. This theory though somewhat modified in practice has been the one adhered to by Great Britain. She has recognized the complete international responsibility of the state in war but when she has recognized non-belligerent rights of enemy subjects it has only been as a concession in behalf of humanity and contrary to her well established rights. Thus until very recently she refused to allow subjects of enemy states any status in her courts. She is today the firmest opponent of the movement to abolish the practice of capturing enemy private property at sea and though she asserts that prize of war belongs to the state, in practice she still gives it all to the captors thus letting the individual have a very real personal interest in the war. England now, of course, recognizes the rights of enemy non-belligerents required by various international agreements.

b. Reprisal.

2. The right of private reprisal can only be exercised under specific commission from the state.

"And indeed, says Blackstone, this custom of reprisals seems dictated by nature herself for which reason we find in the most ancient times very notable instances of it. But here the necessity is obvious of calling in the sovereign power to determine when reprisals may be made; else every private sufferer would be a judge in his own cause."

In his work on international law Phillimore gives rules for reprisal in time of peace, saying that the sovereign alone can grant the right of reprisal and only goods sufficient to satisfy the debt can be taken, the rest must be returned. Matters of private reprisal can not be adjudicated in prize courts, which are only called into existence by regular war, but come under the jurisdiction of the regular courts of admiralty. The matter is now purely theoretic in England since by the declaration of Paris of 1856 privateering and consequently the right of private reprisal was abolished. No commission for this purpose could now be issued and any one engaged in it would be considered a pirate. Public reprisal is still used as a method of coercion short of war and may be employed for the collection of private debts or for obtaining satisfaction for torts of the individual, though only vessels of the regular navy can take part, according to the declaration of Paris.

The right of reprisal for private redress in time of peace or special reprisal should be distinguished from the right of reprisal during war or general reprisal, sometimes distinguished as the right of Marque. Formerly vessels were commissioned by letters of Marque and reprisal to prey on the general commerce of the enemy to any extent and wherever found during war. This right was only legal under special commission of the sovereign though England seems to have taken a very lenient attitude in dealing with non-commissioned captors even granting them a share of their prizes. Her attitude seems to have been that subjects by making captures without commission offended against municipal law but not against international law. Thus she was at liberty to deal with them as she chose but the injured alien had no recourse under international law. As a matter of fact if the non-commissioned captors had observed due care in the conduct of the prize they were usually rewarded with prize money on its condemnation. The declaration of Paris which abolished this practice was severely criticized by many English writers on the ground that it robbed England of important belligerent rights and some even doubted whether England was legally bound by it on account of some diplomatic irregularities in signing it. But now there can be little doubt but that privateering is illegal in England though volunteer fleets and subsidized steamship lines which are used by all naval powers, come dangerously near to amounting to the same thing.

c. State Title to Prize.

The title to all prize vests originally in the state.

Phillimore says, "The maxim 'Bello Parta Cedunt Reipublicae,' is recognized by all civilized states. In England all acquisitions of war belong to the sovereign who represents the commonwealth. The Sovereign is the fountain of booty and prize." Holland makes a similar statement: "Most systems of law hold that property taken from an enemy vests primarily in the nation, 'Bello Parta Cedunt Reipublicae'. A rule which is the foundation of the law of booty and prize." The same view has been expressed by the court as follows:

"That prize is clearly and distinctly the property of the crown and the sovereign in this country, the executive government in all countries in whom is vested the power of levying the forces of the state and of making war and peace, is alone possessed of all property in prize, is a principle not to be disputed.—— It is equally clear that the title of a party claiming prize must needs in all cases be the act of the crown, by which the royal pleasure to grant the prize shall have been signified to the subject." But this principle is carried further and even after an express grant of prize money has been made the crown still has exclusive control over prize. In other words the grant of prize money creates no legal right which the captor can maintain against the pleasure or whim of the crown. In the case of "The Elsebe" Sir William Scott said:

"It is admitted on the part of the captors that their claim rests wholly on the order of council, the proclamation and the prize act. It is not denied that independent of these instruments the whole subject matter is in the hands of the crown as well in point of interest as in point of authority. Prize is altogether a creature of the crown. No man has or can have any interest, but what he takes as the mere gift of the crown. Beyond the extent of that gift he has nothing.—— This is the principle of law on the subject and founded on the wisest reasons. The right of making war and peace is exclusively in the crown. The acquisitions of war belong to the crown and the disposal of these acquisitions may be of utmost importance for the purposes both of war and peace. This is no peculiar doctrine of our constitution, it is universally received as a necessary principle of public jurisprudence by all writers on the subject.—— Bello parta cedunt reipublicae—— It is not to be supposed that the wise attribute of sovereignty is conferred without reason; it is given for the purpose assigned that the power to whom it belongs to decided peace or war may use it in the most beneficial manner for the purposes of both. A general presumption arising from these considerations is that the government does not mean to divest itself of this universal attribute of sovereignty conferred for such purposes unless it is so clearly and unequivocally expressed.—— For these reasons the crown has declared that till after adjudication the captor has no interest which the court can properly notice for any legal effect whatsoever." From considerations of public policy the judge considers that the sacrifice of this inalienable right of the crown would be apt to lead to constant international differences or even war and concludes "I am of opinion that all principles of law, all considerations of public policy, concur to support the right of release prior to adjudication which I must pronounce to be still inherent in the crown." As based on policy and international law this decision was no doubt correct and necessary, but it seems more doubtful whether from the standpoint of English law either a court or the royal prerogative can divest a property right which has been unequivocally granted by act of parliament, as appears to have been done in the case of the act here in question. However under the present prize act the crowns rights are expressly reserved so there could now be no question.

It therefore appears that at present England recognizes the absolute title of the crown to all prizes, until after decree of distribution.

d. Adjudication of Prizes.

Distribution should be decreed only after adjudication of the prize by a competent tribunal of the state. Benedict has said "Before property captured can be properly disposed of it must be condemned as prize in a regular judicial proceeding in which all parties interested may be heard."

The letter of Sir J. Nicholl and Sir William Scott to United States Ambassador Jay authoritatively states British opinion. The portion given was quoted by the authors from a report made by a commission to the king in 1753.

"Before the ship or goods can be disposed of by the captors there must be a regular judicial proceeding, wherein both parties may be heard, and condemnation thereupon as prize in a court of admiralty, judging by the law of nations and treaties.

"The proper and regular court for these condemnations is the court of that state to whom the captor belongs.

"If the sentence of the court of admiralty is thought to be erroneous, there is in every country a superior court of review consisting of the most considerable persons to which the parties who think themselves aggrieved may appeal, and the superior court judges by the same rule which governs the court of admiralty, viz. the law of nations, and the treaties subsisting with that neutral power whose subject is a party before them.

"If no appeal is offered it is an acknowledgement of the justice of the sentence by the parties themselves and conclusive.

"In this method all captures at sea were tried during the last war by Great Britain, France, and Spain and submitted to by the neutral powers. In this method by courts of admiralty acting according to the law of nations and particular treaties all captures at sea have immemorially been judged of in every country in Europe. Any other method of trial would be manifestly unjust, absurd and impracticable."

In regard to the competency of courts this subject is now dealt with by statute. It has been judicially stated that no British subject can maintain an action in a municipal court against the captors for prize. The court of admiralty is the proper tribunal and it exercises prize jurisdiction only under special commission from the crown. In 1801 a case arose in which a vessel was condemned as prize and the proceeds distributed by decree of the vice admiralty court of Santo Domingo. It appeared that the court had no commission to act as a prize court. On retrial the British prize court said:

"But the court having no authority those proceedings are nill and of no legal effect whatsoever." In spite of this decision Phillimore expresses the opinion that in the absence of a special commission the regular courts of admiralty could legally exercise prize jurisdiction according to ancient custom. Under the present law there can be no question as to what courts are commissioned. It therefore appears to be established that English jurisprudence demands a judicial adjudication by a duly commissioned court before distribution of prize money.

e. Method of Distribution.

The method of distributing prize money is determined by municipal law.

The statutory regulations and orders in council decreeing the method of distribution in England together with the instructions to naval commanders have already been noted. A brief consideration of their judicial interpretation may throw some additional light on the actual method of determining the shares of prize received by the captors.

Benefit may be received by the captors or destroyers of vessels in three ways. 1. As prize bounty. A special reward is often given for destroying or capturing enemy vessels. Usually it is given only for destroying armed vessels of the enemy though in some cases, bounty has also been given for the destruction of merchantmen. It is a sum of money given from the treasury of the government irrespective of the value of the prize captured. In distributing it an effort is made to determine the strength of the opposing vessel, thus it is given either as gun money, a fixed amount for each gun on the enemy vessel or as head money, a fixed amount for each man on the enemy vessel at the beginning of the engagement. 2. As military salvage. A reward is usually given for the recapture and return of vessels belonging to citizens of their own or allied countries. This reward is of a similar nature to the salvage which is ordinarily paid for the recovery of shipwrecked vessels in time of peace. The amount paid is usually a certain proportion of the total value of the recaptured prize. 3. As prize money. This is the portion of the actual proceeds of the prize captured given to the captors. The amount of benefit in this case would of course depend on the value of the prize captured, and if the prize is destroyed there obviously is no prize money. Formerly money might also be received as ransom, that is a prize would be released by the captors on the giving of a ransom bill which obligated the master of the prize to continue to a certain port, to refrain from future voyages during the war, and to pay a fixed sum of money as ransom. Thus ransom would partake of the nature of prize money and be divided in the same way. The practice was abolished in England in 1782 by statute but seems to have been allowed later in special cases though each succeeding prize statute repeated the prohibition. It is now illegal unless specially authorized by Order in Council under the naval prize act of 1864.

NOTES.

Chapter V, Part 2.

See ante, <u>p. 26</u>.

Op. cit. iii, 77; see also Blackstone, op. cit. i, 257.

On the relation of the individual to the state see Westlake, Principles of International Law, Cambridge, England, 1894, p. 258; Rousseau, The Social Contract, English translation from French, by Tozer, London, 1909, p. 106. The theory associated with the name of Rousseau appears to have been first enunciated by Giustino Gentili in 1690, see C. M. Ferrante, Private Property in Maritime War, Political Science Quarterly, 1895, xx, 708.

Blackstone, op. cit. i, 259.

Phillimore, op. cit. iii.

By the terms of the Giudon de la Mer; the ordinance of Louis XIV, 1681; the treaty of Utrecht, 1713; the treaty of Versailles, 1786; the right of reprisal was to be granted only to those who could prove damages done and when the offending state had refused legal redress. Prizes judged were to be judged in the same way as prize of war and any surplus in excess of the amount claimed was to be returned, Carnazza-Amari, op. cit. ii, 596, compare with English statute of 1416, ante p. 35, and note.

Phillimore, op. cit. iii, 601.

On English opposition to the declaration of Paris see Phillimore, op. cit. iii, 360; T. G. Bowles, Maritime Warfare, London 1878; Robert Ward, Treatise of the Relative Rights and Duties of Belligerent and Neutral Powers in Maritime Affairs, 1801, reprinted with notes on the Declaration of Paris by Lord Stanley of Alderley, London, 1875.

Sir Thomas Barclay, Privateers, Encyclopedia Britannica, 11th Edition, xxii, 370.

Phillimore, op. cit. iii, 209.

T. E. Holland, Jurisprudence, 11th Edition, London, 1910, p. 212.

Lord Chancellor Brougham in Alexander vs Duke of Wellington, 2 Russel and Mylne 54, 1831; quoted in Phillimore, op. cit. iii, 209; Walker,

The Science of International Law, p. 320; Wheaton, International Law, p. 490.

5 C. Rob. 173, 1804, quoted in Atherley-Jones, op. cit. p. 524, Wheaton, International Law, p. 490.

37 Geo. III, c 109, 1797.

E. C. Benedict, The American Admiralty, 4th Edition, Albany, 1910. p. 420.

For full text of letter see, Phillimore, op. cit. iii, 666; Wharton, Digest of the International Law of the United States, 2nd Edition, Washington, 1887, iii, sec. 330; Moore, International Law Digest, Washington, 1906, vii, 603.

Le Caux vs Eden, 2 Doug. 595, 99 Eng. Rep. 375; see also Phillimore, op. cit. iii, 213. As to necessity of a commission to establish a prize court see ante p.

Huldah, 3 C. Rob. 235, quoted in Atherley-Jones, op. cit. p. 521.

Phillimore, op. cit. iii, 655.

See ante <u>p. 73</u>.

22 Geo. iii, c 25, s 1, 2, 1782.

The Ships taken at Genoa, 4 C. Rob. 403; The Hoop, 1 C. Rob. 169, quoted in Phillimore, iii, 644.

27 and 28 Vict., c 25, s 45, 1864; also Holland, Manual of Naval Prize Law, sec. 273.

PART 3. PRIZE BOUNTY.

As previously noted the distribution of bounty is now regulated by statute and proclamation. If awarded in any war it is given as head money of five pounds per man on every enemy armed vessel sunk or destroyed. The sharers of bounty are much more limited than those of prize money. Thus joint or constructive captors do not share and the flag officer if not present has no claim. Only those who actually take part in the conflict share in bounty. Bounty is apportioned among the officers and crew of those vessels sharing, in the same way as prize money, with the exceptions noted above.

NOTES.

27 and 28 Vict., c 25, s 42.

Order in Council, Sept. 17, 1900, see Statutory rules and Orders, Revised 1903, Vol. ix, tit. Navy, p. 112.

PART 4. PRIZE SALVAGE.

Whether or not military salvage is paid depends upon (1) the character of the original captor, whether recognized belligerent or pirate, (2) the character of the original owner of the vessel whether neutral, subject, or ally, (3) the character of the title the original captor has in the vessel.

In regard to the first point it may be said that recaptures from pirates or unrecognized belligerents should always be returned to the original owner on the payment of salvage. Pirates can never acquire any title in a capture, so the title of the original owner remains good. We need therefore consider only recapture from recognized belligerents.

In the case of recapture of neutral vessels the original captor had no title and could get none. A prize court of his own country would have decreed restitution of the vessel to the original owner so the recaptor has conferred no benefit by recapturing the vessel. He therefore is entitled to no salvage. In cases, however where no legal prize court exists in the country of the original captor the recaptor does the original owner benefit so should be rewarded by salvage. This situation was held to have existed in France in 1799 and in a case which came up at that time Sir William Scott speaking for the British prize court said:

"I know perfectly well that it is not the modern practice of the law of nations to grant salvage on recapture of neutral vessels; and upon this plain principle that the liberation of a clear neutral from the hand of the enemy is no essential service rendered to him, inasmuch as that same enemy would be compelled by the tribunals of his own country, after he had carried the neutral into port to release him with costs and damages for the injurious seizure and detention." However in the case before the court the French courts were held to be incompetent so salvage was awarded the captor.

In recapture of vessels originally belonging to subjects, most countries make distinctions in reference to the character of the original captors title. However Great Britain has provided by statute that recaptures shall always revert to the original owner when a subject on payment of salvage with the one exception that in case the vessel has been fitted out by the enemy as a ship of war it shall not be returned but shall be declared good prize.

The final case remains of recaptures of vessels of an ally. Here the question of the original captor's title enters in, for if the original captor had good title, the vessel is enemy property and should be condemned as good prize to the benefit of the recaptor; but if the title of the original captor is incomplete the original owner still has a certain title which must be respected. The question therefore arises, when is the original captor's title complete? There have been many rules on the subject. Thus Sir William Scott has said:

"It can not be forgotten that by the ancient law of Europe the perductio infra praesidia, infra locum tutum was a sufficient conversion of the property, that by a later law a possession of twenty-four hours was sufficient to divest the former owner. This is laid down in the 287th article of the Consolato Del Mare in terms not very intelligible in themselves but which are satisfactorily explained by Grotius and by his commentator Barbeyrac in his notes upon that article." Sir Leoline Jenkins, in 1672 said:

"In England we have not the letter of any law for our direction only I could never find that the court of admiralty either before the late troubles or since has in these cases adjudged the ships of one subject good prize to another." He then refers to the Commonwealth laws of 1649 and says, "Whether the usurpers intended this as a new law or an affirmance of the ancient custom of England I will not take upon me to determine, only I will say, condemnation upon the enemies possession for twenty-four hours is a modern usage." Later legal adjudication and condemnation was clearly required before the title of the captor state was complete. Thus Lord Mansfield said:

"I have talked with Sir George Lee who has examined the books of the court of admiralty and he informs me that they hold the property not changed, so as to bar the owner in favor of a vendee or recaptor till there had been a sentence of condemnation, and that in the reign of Charles II, Sir Richard Floyd gave a solemn judgment upon the property and decided restitution of a ship retaken by a privateer after she had been fourteen weeks in the enemies possession because she had not been condemned." And again "That no property vest in any goods taken at sea or on land by a ship or her crew, till a sentence of condemnation as good and lawful prize." These cases referred to vessels owned by subjects rather than allies as they occurred before the law granting especial restitution to citizens had been passed but they serve to make it clear that English law regards the title of the enemy captor complete and the title of the original owner destroyed after legal condemnation in the enemy prize court and not before. Vessels originally belonging to allies after such condemnation will be considered good prize and the ally has no claim. There is no question of salvage, instead the captor receives his share of prize money. Recaptures before the enemy title is complete revert to the ally on payment of salvage but if instances can be given of British property retaken by them and condemned as prize, the court of admiralty will determine the case according to their own rule.

Thus the recaptor may receive no reward at all, may be entitled to salvage or may be entitled to prize money.

The first case occurs when a neutral vessel is recaptured from a recognized belligerent.

The second occurs when the recapture is made from a pirate, when the original owner is a British subject, or when the original owner is an ally and the vessel has not been condemned by the enemy's prize court.

The third case occurs when the vessel originally belonged to an ally but has been legally condemned by the enemy prize court and in any case of an ally's vessel where that country refuses to return British vessels.

To be entitled to salvage the recaptor must make an actual military recapture. Constructive recaptures such as occupation of a vessel abandoned by the enemy do not entitle to military salvage.

As already stated where salvage is allowed it consists of one-eighth of the value of the vessel and cargo recaptured or in cases of exceptional difficulty one-fourth to be governed by the discretion of the court. Salvage is apportioned among the officers and crew in the same manner as prize money.

NOTES.

Chapter V, Part 4.

The War Onsken, 2 C. Rob. 299, quoted in Atherley-Jones, op. cit. p. 601.

27 and 28 Vict., c 25, s 40, L'Actif, Edw. Adm. Rep. 184, quoted in Atherley-Jones, op. cit. p. 608.

The Ceylon, 1 Dod. Adm. Rep. 105, quoted in Atherley-Jones, op. cit. p. 607.

Sir Leoline Jenkins, Life of, by Wynne, ii, 770; quoted in Atherley-Jones, op. cit. p. 619.

Lucas 79, quoted in Atherley-Jones, op. cit. p. 619.

Lindo vs. Rodney, 2 Doug. 612; 99 Eng. Rep. 385; see also Atherley-Jones, op. cit. p. 619.

The Santa Cruz, 1 C. Rob. 497, quoted in Atherley-Jones, op. cit. p. 622.

Phillimore, op. cit. iii, 638.

27 and 28 Vict., c 25, s 40, 1864.

PART 5. PRIZE MONEY.

Whenever a vessel or cargo is adjudged good prize by the court it is publicly sold and the proceeds are decreed to the captors as prize money, unless they are non-commissioned or forfeit it by failure to observe the regulations imposed upon them for the conduct and safe keeping of the prize. In England the proceeds of all vessels and cargoes, whether of a purely mercantile or of a military character are divided as prize money, though the government reserves the right of preemption on naval and victualling stores. The rules which govern the prize court in adjudging a captured vessel good prize or not are beyond the scope of this paper. In general all enemy vessels are condemned, and neutral vessels are condemned for breach of blockade, carriage of contraband or unneutral service. These matters are at present largely covered by the Hague conventions of 1907 and the Declaration of London of 1909. However as previously noted the crown reserves the right to free any vessel even though its capture was perfectly legal and it was of a class that would ordinarily be adjudged good prize.

In the distribution of prize money there must be decided, first, what vessels are to share in the prize; second, what proportion each vessel is to get, and third, what proportion of the vessels share each officer and man on board is to receive.

The second and third points are settled by the prize proclamation which decrees division among the officers and men of all the vessels sharing according to the grade they occupy. There is no division among the vessels but all men entitled to share are grouped together in eleven grades, each one of which receives a fixed proportion of the prize money. This portion is then divided equally among all the men of that grade, no matter on what vessel they served. Thus a sailor on a vessel constructively assisting receives exactly the same share as a sailor of the same grade on the vessel making the actual capture.

Where some of the vessels are allies the division is usually regulated by treaty. The provisions of Great Britain's treaties with France of 1854 and 1860 have already been noted. In these cases division was to be made between the vessels of the allies according to the number of men on board irrespective of rank. Of course, for the share decreed to her own vessels, England employed her own rules of division. Where there is no treaty or some of the vessels are privateers the division among the vessels is decreed by the court, an effort being made to apportion it according to the relative strength of the vessels. To determine this the number of men, guns or both on the various vessels are considered. Thus Mansfield said,

"The law of nations does not determine but if one might guess at it, it must be in the ratio of the strength of the respective captors, to know which the number of guns, weight of metal, number of men and strength of each fleet must be stated."

The court must decide the first question proposed, namely what vessels were either actual or joint captors and as such entitled to share. In defining these terms the court has said:

"All prize belongs absolutely to the crown which for the last 150 years has been in the habit of granting it to the takers who are of two classes, actual captors and joint or constructive captors. Joint captors are those who have assisted or are taken to have assisted the actual captors by conveying encouragement to them or intimidation to the enemy." It is in general considered that this encouragement or intimidation is given by all vessels in sight but this is not always true. Thus:

"For it is perfectly clear that being in sight of all cases is not sufficient. What is the real and true criteria?—— There must be some actual, constructive endeavor as well as a general intention."

But in the case of king's ships all in sight generally share.

"They are under a constant obligation to attack the enemy whenever seen. A neglect of duty is not to be presumed and therefore from the mere circumstance of being in sight a presumption is sufficiently raised that they are there animo capiendi." This rule holds irrespective of the character of the vessel making the actual capture.

With privateers the case is different:

"For they are not under obligation to fight. It must be shown in their case that they were constructively assisting. The being in sight is not sufficient with respect to them to raise a presumption of cooperation in capture.— There must be the animus capiendi demonstrated by some overt act, by some variation of conduct which would not have taken place but with reference to that particular object and if the intention of acting against the enemy had not been effectually entertained." As privateering has been abolished this rule is now purely theoretical.

These rules are subject to exceptions however as for instance in the case of captures made in the night or after a joint chase. In such cases ships of the navy definitely associated share though not in sight. Thus:

"A fleet so associated is considered as one body unless detached by orders or entirely separated by accident and what is done by one continuing to compose in fact a part of the fleet, enures to the benefit of all."

A vessel shares in the captures of its tenders.

"I apprehend that the tender becomes as has been contended in law a part of the ship to which she has been attached and that any capture made by her enures to the benefit of the ship to which the tender is an adjunct." Tenders are usually non-commissioned vessels but as they are considered agents of a commissioned vessel their captures are good. The same is true of captures made by ships boats but no constructive captures are allowed by boats of other vessels in sight.

Transport vessels do not participate as joint captors. A case involving transports arose in 1799. The court said:

"It has not been shown that these ships set out in an originally military character, or that any military character has been subsequently impressed upon them by the nature and course of their employment and therefore, however meritorious their services may have been and however entitled they may be to the gratitude of their country it will not entitle them to share in this valuable capture."

The division of captures made by joint naval and military expedition are under the jurisdiction of prize courts. So far as possible the same principles of division are employed in dividing proceeds among soldiers of the army as in dividing prize money in the navy. In regard to the conditions that permit a joint land expedition to share the court said in 1799:

"Much more is necessary than a mere being to sight to entitle an army to share jointly with the navy in the capture of an enemy's fleet". A common interest is presumed with naval vessels in sight, not so with the army. "The services must be such as were directly or materially influencing the capture so that the capture could not have been made without such assistance or at least not certainly and without great hazard." The prize act of 1864 now governs the division in joint military and naval captures.

Captures made by non-commissioned ships which now includes all vessels not part of the royal navy go to the government. Such captures were originally one of the Droits of Admiralty but since the office of admiral has been in commission they enure to the crown. Peculiarly enough, though all such forfeitures now go to the crown the technical distinction of condemnation to the king, jure coronae and condemnation to the king in his office of admiralty. Droits of Admiralty is still maintained in the decrees of prize courts. By statute all such Droits of Admiralty and Jure Coronae are now put into the consolidated fund of Great Britain. In practice it has usually happened that the greater part of the proceeds of captures made by non-commissioned captors is given to the captor as a special reward. For this it appears that England does not recognize an international obligation to prevent captures by non-commissioned vessels in time of war. It is hard to reconcile this attitude with her adoption of the Declaration of Paris in 1856. She does not of course issue letters of Marque or officially permit capture by any vessels other than those of the royal navy. England has not been engaged in any important naval war since the treaty of Paris so it is impossible to say exactly what her practice in this regard would be. Legally all rights in captures by non-commissioned captors enure to the crown so if such vessels infringed on neutral rights England would undoubtedly refuse to give them any reward, which would soon have the effect of stopping such captures.

Definite rules are prescribed for the conduct of prizes, as for instance, the cargoes must not be tampered with, the holds must be closed, all necessary papers must be presented with the prize, the prize must be brought in without delay and proceedings must be commenced in the prize court without unreasonable delay.

"It is to be observed that the captors have no right to convert property till it has been brought to legal adjudication. They are not even to break bulk."

"The captor holds but an imperfect right; the property may turn out to belong to others, and if the captor put it in an improper place or keeps it with too little attention he must be liable to the consequences if the goods are not kept with the same caution with which a prudent person would keep his own property."

Negligence on the part of the captors in caring for the prize or infringement of national or international laws on the subject will result in the forfeiture of all share of the prize and indeed as already observed without any fault on the part of the captor the crown may refuse the captors any share by returning the vessel as a matter of policy. This almost always occurs at the close of a war when it is usually provided by treaty that unadjudicated prizes should be returned. The captor's rights in prize are purely at the mercy of the crown. What he receives he receives by the crown's grace and not by legal right.

NOTES.

Chapter V, Part 5.

See post p. 102 to 104.

27 and 28 Vict., c 25, s 38, 1864.

See Higgins, The Hague Peace Conferences, for all international conventions bearing on these points.

See ante p. 82 et. seq.

Statutory Rules and Orders, revised, 1903, tit. Navy, ix. 109.

See ante p. 61 and 62.

Duckworth vs. Tucker, 1809, 2 Taunt. 7, quoted in Atherley-Jones, op. cit. p. 560.

Banda and Kirwee Booty, 1866, 1 Law Rep. Adm. and Ecc. 109, see also Phillimore, op. cit. iii, 222.

The Vryheid, 2 C. Rob. 16, quoted in Atherley-Jones, op. cit. p. 544.

La Flore, 5 C. Rob. 268, quoted, ibid. p. 546.

Amitie, 6 C. Rob. 261, quoted, ibid. p. 546.

Forsigheid, 3 C. Rob. 311, quoted, ibid. p. 546.

The Carl, 2 Spinks 261, quoted, ibid. p. 550.

The Cape of Good Hope, 2 C. Rob. 284, quoted, ibid. p. 556.

The Dordrecht, 2 C. Rob. 55, quoted, ibid. p. 558.

27 and 28 Vict., c 25, s 34, 1864.

"Any ship or goods taken as Prize by any of the officers and crew of a ship other than a ship of war of Her Majesty shall, on condemnation, belong to Her Majesty in Her office of Admiralty." 27 and 28 Vict., c 25, s 39, 1864.

See ante p. 52.

27 and 28 Vict., c 24, s 17; 1 and 2 Vict., c 2, s 2; 1 Edw. VII, c 4, s 1; 10 Edw. VII and 1 Geo. V, c 28, s 1.

The Haase, 1 C. Rob. 286, quoted in Phillimore, op. cit. iii, 601.

For statutory obligations see 27 and 28 Vict., c 25, s 37, for rules of Hollands, Manual of Naval Prize Law, see ante, p. 66.

L'Ecole, 6 C. Rob. 220, quoted in Atherley-Jones, op. cit. p. 524.

Maria and Vrow Johanna, 4 C. Rob. 348, quoted ibid. p. 524.

27 and 28 Vict., c 25, s 37, 1864.

See ante p. 82 et seq.

CHAPTER VI. GREAT BRITAIN, SIGNIFICANCE OF PRESENT LAW.

PART 1. CAUSES OF LAW.

As has been indicated since the beginning of the eighteenth century the principles of prize distribution in England have undergone but little alteration. With the statutes of Anne parliamentary control of prize matters became established and the method at that time adopted of decreeing distribution by order in council authorized by act of parliament has since been followed. The policy of giving all the proceeds of prizes to the captors after legal adjudication before a competent prize court has likewise been adhered to from that time.

By the reign of Anne, England was definitely established as an imperial colonial power. Her Indian empire was founded, her American colonies were flourishing, Marlborough's successful wars gave her great European prestige. This necessitated the establishment of a policy of naval supremacy, a policy which she has since maintained. At the same time she realised her increasing dependence on commerce. Numerous efforts were made to increase British trade at this time through legislation. She understood that law must reign on the sea if commerce was to prosper. While she depended on her navy to protect her trade routes, she recognized that she could not protect them from the cruisers of all the world and so sought to respect neutral rights. This necessity was realized slowly. During the eighteenth century in pursuing her aggressive naval policy England several times offended neutral powers as for instance by the rule of 1756 but in the main neutral rights were respected and prizes were not taken or distributed except with the strict sanction of law.

Thus as in former periods England's military policy has been influenced by the two factors, commercial dependence and naval aggressiveness. The interests of the former have compelled her to respect neutral rights and maintain strict legality in all her war-like measures. As reflected in her prize law it has brought about powerful legal control of prize matters through prize courts of great authority and unfailing justice. It has forced the crown to assert its primal right to all prizes that it may restore them if policy demands. It has put all prize law under the control of parliamentary statutes, directing the policy of the law but has left the government wide discretion in arranging the details to suit the exigencies of a particular conflict.

The interests of the latter have impelled her to assert belligerent rights to the utmost. England has always been the most reluctant of all nations to abandon an established belligerent right at sea. Thus she still gives the whole of the proceeds of legally captured prizes to the captors for the purpose of encouraging seamen, and increasing the efficiency of the navy.

NOTES.

Chapter VI, Part 1.

For English regard for commerce see Blackstone, I, 260; "Indeed the law of England as a commercial country pays very particular regard to foreign merchants in innumerable instances." He also quotes Montesquieu, Esprit des Lois, XX, 13; "That the English have made the protection of foreign merchants one of the articles of their national liberty." See also navigation Acts of 1650, Scobell, 152, of 1651, Scobell, 176, of 1660, 12 Car. II c 18.

See discussion of the rule of 1756, and England's opposition to the armed neutralities of 1780 and 1800 in Wheaton, History of the Law of Nations. On her opposition to the immunity of enemy property on neutral vessels, see Ward, Treatise on the Rights and Duties of Neutrals, and Bowles, Maritime War. England is today the strongest opponent of the movement to abolish the right to capture enemy private property at sea, see Report of meeting of Institut of International Law, Revue de Droit International, 1875, vii, 275, 329; also official report of the Second Hague Conference.

PART 2. EFFECTS OF LAW.

a. The Navy

To discuss the effects of England's prize money law is a very difficult task. However a few remarks may be made considering the question with reference to its effect, first, on the English navy and second, on international law.

It might be thought that the encouragement of mariners by the hope of private gain would tend to increase the efficiency of the navy and this is the avowed purpose of distribution in all the statutes authorizing it. England has undoubtedly always had a very efficient navy but she has almost always found it necessary to use the press gang to man her vessels in her important naval wars. The hope of prize money has not been sufficient to furnish enough volunteers to fill the navy.

In connection with privateering there can be no doubt but that the generous giving of prizes has enabled England to make effective war with little national expense. Elizabeth's wars cost her nothing, rather they were a source of income. The same was true of the wars of the eighteenth century. The hope of gain seemed always sufficient to enlist private enterprise in privateering war. However privateering is now abolished. Modern naval strategy demands a few men-of-war rather than many cruisers. Captain Mahan considers commercial war as of comparatively small importance. An effective blow can only be struck by conflict with the enemy's armed vessels. Any amount of commerce destroying can not conclude the war in his opinion, though he by no means takes the stand that commerce destroying should be abolished. It would seem that the small share of prize which might possibly be received by a sailor in a modern ship would be a negligible factor in increasing naval efficiency. Rather it would be a deterrent as it would attract vessels into commercial war instead of into the more effective conflicts with the enemy's armed vessels. With the abolition of privateering it would seem that the value of prize money as a means of increasing the efficiency of the navy departed.

b. International Law.

England's prize money laws can not be said to have imperiled neutral rights. England has always insisted on the most extreme belligerent rights but it can not be said that her courts often denied a neutral right that was really established by international law. The prize courts of Mansfield and Stowell have been considered models of fairness throughout the world. Though the utmost privileges were given to privateers and the sailors of the royal navy the even handed justice of the prize courts fully protected neutral rights by restoring illegal captures made with the hope of private gain. With a people of less law abiding disposition and less used to submission to law than the English this might not be true.

It might be supposed that the generosity toward the captors of prize would be calculated to decrease the destruction of prizes at sea. If the prize were destroyed of course the captor would obtain no prize money. English publicists are inclined to admit the right of destruction at sea. Thus Scott, Lushington and Holland say that it should not be resorted to except in cases of extreme urgency but on occasion it may be justifiable or even praiseworthy. Continental writers on the contrary are inclined to disallow entirely the legality of the destruction of prizes. Bluntschli and Heffter greatly deprecate the practice. In spite of the apparent authority for such action given by English publicists English cruisers have very seldom destroyed prizes. This may be due partly to her prize money law but probably to a greater extent to her widely scattered territories which make it almost always possible to get a prize to an English port. At present the destruction of neutral prizes is closely circumscribed by the provisions of the Declaration of London on that point so it is not likely that the abolition of prize money would bring about an increase in this practice.

The movement toward the abolition of the right to capture enemy private property at sea, historically advocated by the United States, is coming into increasing favor in England, though England as a nation always has been and still is the leading opponent of the innovation. As pointed out above, modern naval strategy deprecates commercial war as also does humanitarianism. A considerable number of English publicists are now advocating the abolition of this right not only on behalf of humanity but also as a matter of wise military policy for Great Britain. The increasing importance of unrestrained commerce to the island has influenced many to believe that England would gain more than she would lose by the abandonment of this belligerent right.

It may be useful to consider how much effect the institution of prize money has upon England's attitude on this question. There is no doubt but that sailors and officers of the navy like to get prize money. There is the gambler's zest to money received in this way and undoubtedly the personnel of the navy would offer all the resistance in their power to the abolishment of prize money. A section in the proposed prize act of 1910 illustrates this.

The act was offered in order to permit of the appeal of prize cases to the international prize court provided for by the Hague conference of 1907. The section in question authorized the admiralty to give prize money on estimated value even when the prize was liberated by the court. The object of this section was evidently to insure reward to the captors in case of a possible undue liberality on the part of the international prize court, and would seem to imply a certain lack of confidence in that court. This bill was lost with little discussion. However, the provision indicates that the element favoring prize money is ready to push its interests in legislation.

If the war right of capturing private enemy property at sea were abandoned the chance of getting prize money would automatically disappear except in the comparatively rare cases of contraband and breach of blockade. Is the naval sentiment in favor of prize money strong enough to keep England from falling in with other nations in this movement toward abolishing the right of capture at sea? It does not seem likely. The selfish, personal desires of a small portion of the population can not be sufficient to sway the policy of a great nation like England if broader considerations demand a change. England's resistance to the movement for abolishing the right to capture private property at sea can be traced to other causes. John Stuart Mill once called the right to attack commerce "our chief defensive weapon." Phillimore, Twiss, Westlake, and Lorimer all favored the retention of the right. It is idle to suppose that these men had no stronger reason for their stand than that it permitted seamen to get prize money. From the standpoint of military science there has been in the past justification for the retention of this right by England, and many sincerely believe that even now England must retain it as a military defense.

In the vote on the American proposition for abolishing this right of capture taken at the Second Hague conference the prize money laws of the different countries apparently had no effect on their vote. Italy and Sweden who give prize money as well as the United States and Germany who do not favored the resolution. On the other hand, Japan who has never given prize money voted against the proposal as also did Great Britain, France and Russia who have always given it. It should be remembered that the United States advocated the abolition of the right to capture private property at sea for a century before she abolished prize money. Italy also has consistently advocated that policy since 1870 though she still gives prize money. It does not seem that the local law of prize money has any great effect on the countries attitude on the question of the right to capture private property at sea.

As stated there is a growing movement in England in favor of abandoning the right of capturing private property at sea. The discussion has been entirely based on considerations of broad national policy. The existence of prize money has not entered into the matter. It does not seem likely that England's laws of prize money have had or do now have any appreciable influence on her attitude in this question.

c. Conclusion.

It seems that under present conditions the giving of prize money in England has little effect either for good or evil. Since the abolition of privateering it appears to have had little value in increasing the efficiency of the navy or in decreasing the expense of war. Neutral rights have not been imperiled by it for in England it has not given rise to biased judgment on illegal captures. While it may have decreased the destruction of prizes before adjudication it does not appear likely that its abandonment would now have any effect on this matter. Neither does it seem probable that it has had much influence in determining England's stand on the question of the right to capture private enemy property at sea.

In view of this inoffensive character of prize money in England it is not surprising that it remains law. Sailors and naval officers want to keep it. The institution is long established in custom by which the English are proverbially bound. Unless a definite charge can be brought against it, it does not seem likely that the present practice will be abolished. England's stand at the Hague conference of 1907 seemed to indicate this attitude. On that occasion a proposition was introduced by the French delegation to abolish prize money. It was offered as a substitute to the American plan of abolishing the right to capture private property at sea. Great Britain opposed the scheme. Sir Ernest Satow, the British delegate, said that England could not agree to the proposition as the English parliament had reasons for believing in their present custom of distribution. The reasons, he did not give. He added that he considered the matter as being one solely for internal settlement and not one of international law. We may therefore expect prize money to remain as an institution of British policy, though its influence on international law seems to be very slight.

On theoretical grounds the practice seems to have little basis for existing. It is not in harmony with the modern view of war which seeks so far as possible to eliminate the element of personal gain and to limit the operations of war to strictly state agencies. It encourages war on commerce. Its use savors of privateering. It offers a constant temptation for infringing neutral rights by making illegal captures. With the abolition of privateering and the present views of naval strategy its usefulness as an encouragement for seamen and a means of increasing the efficiency of the navy have departed. It accentuates the gambler's chance which is contrary to all modern ethics. Sailors, the same as soldiers, should receive fixed pay for their services, and not be compelled to rely for their salaries, in part at least, upon the uncertain chance of prize money. Bentwich says of prize money: "The present custom of dividing among the captors the proceeds of sale after adjudication of a prize court preserves in maritime war that taint of belligerent greed and of interested attack upon private property which is against the spirit of modern warfare and which has been declared illegal in land operations."

Though prize money as given in England was an institution of great international importance in the balmy days of privateering especially during the reign of Elizabeth when it was largely responsible for the romantic careers of England's empire builders, for the wholesale capture of Spanish galleons and for England's naval supremacy, it does not seem to have been of any particular importance to any one outside of the naval service of Great Britain since the abolition of privateering. Practically it is valueless. Theoretically it is bad. It should be abolished.

NOTES.

Chapter VI, Part 2.

Common Law fully admits the legality of pressing sailors into service, see Blackstone, I, 419.

Influence of Sea Power upon History, pp. 132-138; Lord Palmerstone also deprecated the value of commercial war, Political Science Quarterly, 1905, xx, 711.

Atherley-Jones, op. cit. 529, 534.

Atherley-Jones, op. cit. 530.

The Declaration of London, Chap. iv. The Declaration of London however is not officially ratified by Great Britain, see Bentwich, The Declaration of London.

England's delegates, Messrs. Twiss, Westlake, Lorimer, and Bernard gave the only dissenting votes to the proposition favoring the abolition of the right to capture private property at sea, Institute of International Law at its meeting at the Hague in 1875, see Revue de Droit International, 1875, vii, 288. England also opposed the proposition at the Second Hague Conference, in 1907, see Second Hague Conference, Acts and Documents, iii, 832.

Among English Publicists favoring the abolition of the right to capture private property at sea may be mentioned Lawrence, Hall and Maine. The question came before the house of commons by motion of Sir John Lubbock, March 22, 1878, but was negatived without division. (See Phillimore, op. cit. iii, 361.) Lord Palmerstone once said, "Question Statesmen, none will tell you that the depredations of privateers have ever decided the success or final result of a war." (See Political Science Quarterly, 1905, xx, 711) and in a speech of 1856 he hoped for the abolition of the right to capture private property at sea. (See Speech by Rufus Choate, Second Hague Conference, Acts and Documents, iii, 770.) Among English publicists on the opposite side are Phillimore, Westlake, T.C. Bowles, Twiss, Lorimer, Sir Shurston Baker, and Norman Bentwich. John Stuart Mill in a letter to the Times, March 11, 1871 spoke of abandonment of the right to capture private property, as "the abandonment of our chief defensive weapon—the right to attack an enemy in his commerce." (See Phillimore, op. cit. 361.) However, in a speech in 1867 he had apparently countenanced the reform, (See Speech of Rufus Choate, Second Hague Conference Acts and Documents, iii, 770.)

Section 21 of the proposed act. For text of this act see Bentwich, The Declaration of London, 174.

Political Science Quarterly, 1905, xx, 711, see also note 7 above.

The full result of the vote was as follows: Aye—Germany, United States, Austria-Hungary, Belgium, Brazil, Bulgaria, China, Cuba, Denmark, Equador, Greece, Hayti, Italy, Norway, Netherlands, Persia, Roumania, Siam, Sweden, Switzerland and Turkey,—21; Nay—Columbia, Spain, France, Great Britain, Japan, Mexico, Montenegro, Panama, Portugal, Russia, Salvador—11; Not Voting, Chile.

For attitude of United States and other countries on this question see speech by Andrew D. White, at the first Hague Conference, (Holls, The Peace Conference at the Hague) and speech by Rufus Choate at the Second Hague Conference, (Second Hague Conference, Acts and Documents, iii, 770.)

The French proposition was as follows: "Considering that, as the law of nations still positively admits the legality of the right of capture, applied to private enemy property at sea, it is eminently desirable that, until a binding agreement is established between states on the subject of suppression, the exercise of it be subordinated to certain modifications.

"Considering, that it is necessary to the above point that, conforming to the modern conception of war that it ought to be directed against states and not against individuals, the right of capturing private property apply only as a means of coercion practiced by a state against a state;

"That in view of these ideas all the individual benefit to the profit of agents of the state which exercises the right of capture ought to be excluded and that the loss suffered by individuals from the taking of prize ought to be finally borne by the state to which they belong;

"The French delegation has the honor of proposing to the fourth commission that it express the wish that states which exercise the right of capture appropriate the portion of prizes given to the crews of the capturing vessels and promulgate the necessary measures, so that the loss, caused by the exercise of the right of capture, will not rest entirely upon the individuals from whom the wealth may have been captured."—This "Voeu" known as annexe 16 of the fourth commission appears in French text in Second Hague Conference Acts and Documents, iii, 1148; English translation in Westlake, International Law, ii, 313. For discussion of the measure see Second Hague Conference, Acts and Documents, iii, 792, 809, 842, 845, 906, 909. Before a vote was taken the two portions of the motion were separated. The final result as given on page 909 of the volume cited was as follows:

On Abolition of prize money; Aye—Germany, Austria-Hungary, Chile, China, France, Greece, Italy, Japan, Montenegro, Norway, Holland, Persia, Russia, Servia, Sweden, Turkey, 16. Nay—United States, Argentina, Cuba,

Mexico, 4. Not Voting—Belgium, Brazil, Denmark, Dominican Republic, Equador, Spain, Great Britain, Hayti, Panama, Paraguay, Portugal, Salvador, Siam, Switzerland, 14.

On State insurance against private loss; Aye—Austria-Hungary, France, Great Britain, Montenegro, Holland, Russia, Servia, 7. Nay—Germany, United States, Argentina, Chile, China, Cuba, Italy, Japan, Mexico, Norway, Persia, Sweden, Turkey, 13. Not Voting—Belgium, Brazil, Denmark, Dominican Republic, Equador, Spain, Greece, Hayti, Panama, Paraguay, Portugal, Salvador, Siam, Switzerland, 14.

Although the United States has abolished prize money, her delegates voted against the proposition on this occasion on the grounds that it was a matter for internal regulation, and that they did not wish to take the emphasis from the broader project of total abolition of the right to capture private property which they advocated. Though England abstained from voting, her delegate expressed opposition to the "Voeu" in debate.

Second Hague Conferences, iii, 906.

Bentwich, The Law of Private Property in War, p. 72.

Milton Keynes UK
Ingram Content Group UK Ltd.
UKHW030626061024
449204UK00004B/273

9 789362 519955